THE DARK SIDE THAT BIRTHED MY WORSHIP

My Story My Journey My Victory

LATOYA L. WALLACE

The Darkside that Birthed my Worship
By Latoya L Wallace
Published by Latoya L Wallace
http://www.latoyalwallace.com

All rights reserved. No parts of this publication may be reproduced, distributed, or transmitted in any form or by any means, including photocopying, recording, or other electronic or mechanical methods, without the prior written permission of the publisher, except at provided by United States of America copyright law.

Printed in the United States of America

Unless otherwise stated all scriptures is taken from the New Living Translations. Public Domain https://www.biblegateway.com/ https://www.biblestudytools.com/

Dictionary references are from:
https://www.webmd.com/skin-problems-and-treatments/guide/vitiligo-common-cause-loss-skin-pigment
Medical News Today Article (September 26, 2017)

https://www.medicalnewstoday.com/articles/245081.php

Graphic Design Cover Illustrator: Ezekiel Williams
Book Cover Design: Jared Araujo
Formatter: Tiffany A Green
Edited by William Rose

THE DARK SIDE THAT BIRTHED MY WORSHIP

Disclaimer: For privacy reasons some names of individuals have been changed

The Darkside that Birthed my Worship
Copyright 2019 Latoya L Wallace
All rights reserved
ISBN: 978-0-578-47673-5

CONTENTS

Dedication 5

Acknowledgements 7

Introduction 11

Chapter 1 Moments 18

Chapter 2 Back to School Different 27

Chapter 3 Now I know (There's no cure) 37

Chapter 4 Safe Haven 43

Chapter 5 The Make Up 52

Chapter 6 The Dance 60

Chapter 7 On to a New Journey (High School) 72

Chapter 8 The Birthing (1st Encounter) 82

Chapter 9 The Turning Point 88

Chapter 10 Rejection on Another Level 102

Chapter 11 I Almost Let Go 113

Chapter 12 The Findings 122

Chapter 13 Just the Two of Us 129

Chapter 14 Hope Again. Finally Liberated 135

Chapter 15 A Love Story 151

Chapter 16 Now it all Makes Sense 157

MY DEDICATION
I WILL NEVER LET YOU GO

To the love of my life, Andre, my husband and best friend. I will always honor you, as well as thank you for the 22 years of love and support you have shown me until the day God called you home. You were by my side through my young adult years and never left. You were there to watch me blossom into the woman I am today. You were my number one supporter. You are the father of my children and an amazing one at that. You were my protector, provider, and my security blanket. I thank God that at my lowest moment in life, when I lost all hope in love, when I knew in my mind that no one would see past my outer appearance, you did. You found me when I was broken and put me back together. You have supported me in all my endeavors, even in those that didn't make sense. Your love for me was expressed in special unique ways and I am going to miss those unexpected surprises you did just to make me smile. Throughout this journey of writing, you passionately stayed up some night waiting on me, you lost sleep by pushing me to finish and you put up with all my moody ways. When I wanted to put it down you were there to fuss and talk me into to picking the pen back up and finish. You were my Balance. I honor you as my husband, for never giving up on me, and allowing me to be me. I will always love you and you will never be forgotten. I salute you, my King.

Mr. Wallace, I dedicate this Book to you
MY FOREVA BOI

ACKNOWLEDGEMENTS

I give all glory and honor to GOD for being the Lord of my life. He loves me more than I love myself. He chose me in my mother's womb. He created uniquely, made me for this season and time to share my story. Humbly Grateful

To my daughter D'Tora, I love you so much. You are my first, and for a while, it was just you and me against the world. When no one else could fulfill the void in my heart, you did. When no one else could wipe my tears, you laid your hand on my face as a baby, and I knew everything would be okay. I had you as a late teen. I walked across the stage eight months pregnant with you in my womb. You have grown into a beautiful, strong young lady. Now you are a mother and a beautiful one at that. You have achieved so much, and the best is yet to come. Thank you for being my daughter. Go as high as you can with God first. Reach beyond the stars and live for my "Ma Lady". She is so proud of you, and so am I.

Thank you.

To my loving son D'Andre, you have the gift of laughter, and you truly are special to me. I thank God for giving me a son. You are very strong-minded and have the gift for talking. I believe you can be a great debater. I want you to go as far in life as the stars. I want you to always aim for the sky. Most importantly, I want your heart to always remain humble. If you do that, God will always make provisions for you. I thank you for being my son.

Thank you.

To my Chunk Munk, Ma'Rae, I will always speak decree and declare greatness over you. You are a world changer. You are so intelligent and such a smart young lady. Every day, you bring joy and peace to the world and those around you. You are the glue that keeps us together. I love you, my little Princess. I thank you for teaching me something new every day. You are great, and you carry the heart of God.

Thank you.

I would also like to thank my parents. You are the reason I exist in this world. I thank God for your strength and endurance as parents. Guiding me and doing all you can to protect me from the ugliness in the world. Mom, you brought me to church and introduced me to Jesus, and I have been in love ever since. Dad, our bond will never be broken. Your smile is what assured me that everything would be alright. As we went through this process together, I thank you that you never gave up on me as your daughter.

THE DARK SIDE THAT BIRTHED MY WORSHIP

Thank you.

My brothers, Louis and Pierre, thank you for being my protectors in school and growing up. I didn't have to fight a lot because you both did all the fighting for me. Most importantly, you tried with everything you had to protect my heart from the pain, hurt and ugliness this world had to offer. Even though you couldn't protect me from all of it, you did a darn good job of just being there as my brothers.

Thank you.

To my Apostle Deon Hill, I thank you, not for just being my shepherd but for filling the shoes of Rev. Weatherspoon and taking me under your wings and grooming me to be the prophet I am today. You have watched me grow in God from a little girl. You have been there for all the important moments in my family's life. You are not only my apostle; I can call you friend. Your godly love is unconditional. I thank you for being a covering, for the wisdom, teachings, impartations, knowledge, and most of all, allowing God in me shine.

Thank you.

INTRODUCTION

You know, it's funny how God works. I would have never thought in a million years, that I would be sharing a part of my life that I once buried. This part of my life was buried forever, so I thought. Clearly, God's plan is not ours, just as He says in His word. Growing up, I learned how to smile through it all. I learned how to suppress the emotions and feelings that were screaming to come out of me. I built this wall. This wall I thought I was protecting myself from the world, but instead I was keeping this little girl inside.

When you think of a wall being placed in front of you, you think of something that is there to confine you. Imagine a space that would hold you back or block something from getting to you, maybe even prevent you from getting to it. For a long time, this little girl lived inside of me. This little girl lived behind that wall. Inside of my heart and mind this little girl dwelled inside of me.

This little girl was emotionally drained. I was this little girl that was sad all the time, but on the outside, I smiled. I was hurting, and my heart was aching. Because this little girl was I and I couldn't let the little girl come out, I created this dark space inside of me. This dark side of me was an ugly, cold and lonely space that she often stayed in. For many years, I learned to live with her buried inside of

THE DARK SIDE THAT BIRTHED MY WORSHIP

me. This dark space was a place in my mind that allowed her to be free. Sounds crazy, I know. as you continue to read, you will find out more about this little girl and the space she occupied within me. Because this little girl lived inside of me, I had to go back to the space she once dwelled to set her free.

> ***Jeremiah 29:11 (NLT) For I know the plans I have for you, says the LORD. They are plans for good and not for disaster, to give you a future and a hope.***

God knew there was going to come a time where I would be reliving a part of my life that I thought I was already set free from. He knew that for me to be totally free, I would have to revisit this place again. But this time, it was not to hear the little girl's voice but to set her completely free. He knew that for others to become free, I first had to be liberated. In my time of writing, some things I thought I once buried came back to life. Feelings I thought were gone and forgotten came back to life. They resurfaced as if they never left. People I thought I forgave I didn't. Things I thought I let go, I found out I was still holding on to them. We would like to believe the saying that says "as time passes it heals all wounds". But it doesn't. It only allows the root to remain until something comes along to bring it back to life.

I invite you to take a journey with me. I will share several experiences and encounters that I went through. How I was able to conquer them all from the place of darkness. There was a time in my life I thought that could never happen. There was a time in my life where I thought I would never come to a place to say I am FREE. There was a time in my life I thought my voice would never be heard and the mental torment would completely take over my mind. While taking this journey with me, my prayer is that you will come to an understanding of God's love. That love that is unfailing.

***Psalms 36:7 How precious is your unfailing love, O God!
All humanity finds shelter in the shadow of your wings.***

God loves us so much; he will come and rescue us in the deepest and darkest times of our lives. Sometimes when you are in the dark, it can appear to be so black there is no trace of light anywhere. In the dark, you seem lost, alone, and feel you will never find your way out. The word Dark according to Merriam-Webster means: devoid or partially devoid of light: not receiving, reflecting, transmitting, or radiating. If there is little to no presence of light, how can one find their way out? This is how the worshipper in me was birth. We know the Bible tells us in

THE DARK SIDE THAT BIRTHED MY WORSHIP

John 4:24 NLT For God is a spirit, and they that worship Him must worship Him in spirit and in truth.

Well, how do we get to that place? How do we get to the place of living a lifestyle of worship? I believe this means to live for God with our heart, mind, and soul. Living a surrendered life devoted to God. Although it sounds easy to do, I believe it is so hard to maintain without obedience. As you read, I will share some intimate truth that has never been told. I'm going to share some transparent moments which will reveal the dark side that allowed the birthing of the worshipper inside of me. When you think of a baby inside the womb of the mother, they are in a dark womb waiting for the appointed time to come out into the light. It must be at the appointed time; it can't be too soon, and it can't be too late. While this little soul is in the womb, it is growing and getting the nourishment needed for its development while in this dark space. When the time is right or at the appointed time, this baby begins to make its way to the light. Once the baby is ready to be birth, this baby comes into the world with the abilities and bodily functions to be able to live in the earth. Well, this is my story of how God rescued me from the inner torment of darkness through the heart of a little girl and birth the worshipper within.

My story is unique because I am unique. My story may seem the same to some but very different to so many. See, I was born with a rare disorder. For many years, a small percentage of the population was diagnosed with this disorder. According to the Medical News Today Globally there are between 0.5 and 2 percent of people that are affected by this disorder. The name of this disorder is called Vitiligo. Vitiligo results from the loss of melanocytes. These are the skin cells that produce melanin, the pigment that gives skin, hair and eyes its color. Vitiligo usually starts as small areas of pigment loss that spread and become larger with time, according to the American Vitiligo Research Foundation. The exact cause of Vitiligo is unclear but there are a few factors that are believed to be triggers that contribute to this disorder. One is an autoimmune disorder, in which the immune system becomes overactive and destroys the melanocytes. It could be a genetic oxidative stress imbalance that could trigger the cells to attack. It could run in the family. Exposure to some chemicals could be a factor. Again, the exact cause is unknown. To my knowledge none of the above has been a factor in my case. At one point, we tried tracing it back through my family tree to figure out where it would have started or where the gene would have come from. I was told that my great

THE DARK SIDE THAT BIRTHED MY WORSHIP

grandfather had this disorder, but I can't be certain because he passed on before I was born. As of today, no living relative of my family has this disorder. This is what makes me unique from anyone in my family. I believe this is what qualified me to be the chosen vessel to tell my story and to share my journey.

So, I invite you to come and take a journey with me. In this book, you will see how the Father rescues me from ultimately myself. I will take you back to a moment in my life that was the darkest times of my years of growing up. By taking this journey, you will begin to see how the love of my Father, our Father will take you and wrap you in His arms. Right when you get to a place you have convinced yourself that one day, it would be the place you would die. As you take this journey with me, my prayer is that you would begin to search your own heart for that dark place that is slowly pulling you in. That you would search deep down for that little girl or little boy that you thought you had buried and begin to set him or her free. My prayer is that after going on this journey with me you will allow God to birth out of you the life within you once thought you would never be able to live. Lastly, my prayer is that once you finish reading this book, the authentic worshipper in you will come alive and be birthed.

CHAPTER 1
MOMENTS

When one thinks of a moment, one would say that it is something that is temporary, something that should only last for a short period of time. Eventually, when that moment is over, it should never come back again. A "moment" according to the Webster dictionary is "a comparatively brief period of time." For me, this moment changed my life forever. This moment was more like a life-altering moment. Growing up as the middle child was not always a good thing. Some think it is the best of both worlds. There were some good days, but there were a lot of not so good days. There were many times I wished I could turn back the hands of time. I am the only girl in my immediate family. I have two brothers, and I am the middle child. I often like to think I am the oldest, but my brothers would always tell me differently. Although for some reason, probably because I was the middle child, I got the most attention when it came to my mother. Being the middle child and the only girl. I was not the most favored. I honor my mother and father and respect them to the utmost. What I am simply saying is she was much harder on me than my brothers. I caught the most hell growing up from her. This caused me to have a very strained

THE DARK SIDE THAT BIRTHED MY WORSHIP

relationship with my mother. The reason I am pointing this out is when the moment that changed my life, I didn't have her as the mother that I needed her to be. My father was a hardworking man. He would leave every morning for work and come home just in time for dinner. Those days were special as a family at one point. I remember the times when my dad would come home, we would sit at the dinner table and eat together. One thing we didn't do as much was share or talk to each other about our day or things that bothered us. We never expressed our feelings in a way that mattered to one another. My brothers would make a lot of jokes and things like that, and we would laugh a lot but nothing beyond that at the dinner table. I didn't have that in the house I grew up in. It just wasn't a normal thing. When that moment came, I didn't know what to say or do because I never felt like a door was opened for me to do so.

    I can remember that moment like it was yesterday. I will never forget the first time I noticed it. One day I was getting ready to go outside and play with my cousins who stayed next door, I stood in front of the mirror combing my hair, and I noticed this white spot on my right index finger I think my first reaction was as if it was going to go away. For a moment, I thought I burned myself with the curling iron and didn't realize it. Yep, it was something that looked so natural, as if it was a birthmark. Shortly, after I notice it, I found myself scratching this area a lot. It started bothering me. It was small, but it was big enough for me to notice it, and it seemed like it was growing out of my cuticle. Again, I thought it was a burn mark on my finger from the curling iron. So, I just kept trying to figure out how did I burn myself and when. I remember showing it to my mother, and she told me it was a rash and that it would go away. So, I did as any child would do, wait until it went away. I found myself scratching the back of my neck a lot as well. Not sure if I did all the time but after noticing the patch on my finger, I began to notice how my neck started bothering more. I took a mirror and saw another spot at the back of my neck. It was very small, and it was red. Again, I'm thinking it's the curling iron. I thought the relaxer had given me a bad rash by this small patch being on my neck. When a relaxer touches that area, the chemicals would burn my skin so bad, I would have sores in that area. At one point, my mother took me to the doctor to see about the area on my neck, and the doctor said it was a chemical infection. After some medicine, what seemed like a rash went away. I didn't notice any redness, and I wasn't scratching it so hard anymore. Then I began

THE DARK SIDE THAT BIRTHED MY WORSHIP

to notice the small patch on my index finger started to get little bigger. Going back to that moment, I started to question myself. I asked myself, "Where did this come from?" Again, I stood there looking at it for a long time. The thought of saying something to my mom kind of went out the window because of her first reaction. Can you imagine being a little girl and a thing starts happening to your body, and you have no one that can explain to you what's going on. This patch all of a sudden appeared out of nowhere. It was small patch, but it wasn't there a year ago. I was in the sixth grade when the process started. It was almost the end of the school year, and I was getting ready for the summer. I had no clue that my life was changing right before my eyes. I mean, who would? I was just a kid. I tried to block it out of my mind. Maybe because I was trying to believe that it was not there maybe, I thought it would go away the same way it appeared. I found myself staring at my finger even more. I was so puzzled because I tried to figure out how and when did I burn my finger and why it wasn't going away. Instead of going to my parents about it, I was in a place of either denial or shock. Either way, I didn't say a word to my parents about it. Well, initially I didn't. The other thing I found myself doing was scratching that area where the doctor told my mother it was an infection all over again. I took a mirror and looked at it again thinking maybe the rash came back, but the spot wasn't red this time but white. At this point, I started to shake. I could feel the tears forming in my eyes. I remember this overwhelming emotion came upon me that caused me to be so frightened. I was literally freaking out. I could see this same white patch that was on my finger now forming on the back on my neck.

I had no choice but to say something to them. I'm sure they knew but then again maybe not. Imagine how I felt as a little girl. When I came to my mother and showed her my finger and neck, she told me she noticed it after the neck rash. I couldn't understand why she never said anything to me about what she had already seen on my body. Maybe they were trying to figure out what was wrong with me and didn't want me to worry or be frightened about it. I don't know. Maybe they were trying to act as if nothing was wrong and it will all go away. I have concluded that they just didn't know what to do. I can't remember them showing concern at the beginning. I don't think my parents understood what I was dealing with or what was happening to me. This may be the reason why no feelings were expressed. My parents were not the compassionate type either.

THE DARK SIDE THAT BIRTHED MY WORSHIP

(Darkness arising)

Now there was a side growing at the same time the white patches were growing. I didn't notice this side at first. It was so subtle and silent. When you think of it, it was like an infection. You know how you don't realize you have an infection growing in you until it gets very bad. This thing was growing on the inside of me. I called it a "hole within." This hole within was getting bigger and darker. No one knew of this inner hole. It wasn't visible to the world, only to me. The definition of a black hole: "a celestial object that has a gravitational field so strong that light cannot escape it and that is believed to be created especially in the collapse of a very massive star." This was growing inside of me. A side that no one could see, but it was slowly eating away at me. It was slowly getting bigger. You may be wondering if I'm talking about my skin, I'm not. I am referring to the inner thing that could fester in your mind and eat away at your thoughts. That dark inner hole that makes you feel empty inside. That dark inner hole that if it goes untreated, one can find themselves never being able to return. Looking back now I can see that it was the spirit of the enemy that got into my mind and formed a voice of reason with my conscience. This is what he does: He will find that weak area to infiltrate. He will begin to plant little seeds, and they will begin to grow. I can remember I would sit and cover my hands or sit on my hands so no one would see the tip of my finger and ask me questions. I would ball my fist up so I would not have to show my index finger. I'm beginning to pay more attention to my skin. I noticed the same white patch on my left index finger. The same pattern started to happen on my left index finger as it did on my right. For some reason, the patch on my left hand wasn't as big as the patch on my right hand. What was happening inside of me was at the time what I called "dysfunction." This may not be the right choice of words, but this is how I felt back then. The name of this disorder is called Vitiligo. Later, I will share with you how I came to know this. It is when the pigment cell of the skin which is melanocyte is destroyed, and it causes white patches to form. The first place I noticed a white patch was on my right index finger. This is where it all began. Everything changed both inside and outside. Now you may think this is nothing, you've been through worse. But for a little girl with everything to look forward to in life, everything changed in just a moment. Remember I told you emotions weren't something that was expressed in our home. I can't tell you when my parents started to notice the patches

THE DARK SIDE THAT BIRTHED MY WORSHIP

getting bigger prior to me showing her, but my parents were starting to pay more attention. I remember at one point my mom told me that her skin did the same thing after she was in a car accident at eighteen years old. This car accident was so bad that it could have ended her life. He protected her, and she survived. From what I understood; this accident caused her to be in the hospital for a very long time. This occurred in Charleston, Mississippi, which was once her hometown. Well, during the time of her accident and her time in the hospital, her pigments went through a lot of changes. She told me her pigment turned black. It was the opposite of what my pigment was beginning to do. I honestly believe this was her way of comforting me. She made me believe this was something temporary and not permanent. That this was just a phase I was going through. Not understanding what was happening to me, but it was a passive way of dealing with the situation. I remember her telling me it was nothing to worry about. I remember talking with my granny here in Chicago and showed her my fingers. She looked at them for a moment and then told me she has the same patch on her legs. I was shocked at first because I thought I was the only one in my entire family that had this issue. I asked her where they did come from, and she replied, "Old age." I laughed because I was only eleven years old at the time. I was far from old age. It seemed nobody was taking this seriously. No one was concerned about it, except it was a huge deal. For me, it was my life. For me, it was not getting the answer I was searching for. For me, it was, "Why is this happening to me?" For me, it was, "What the hell is this?" These were the thoughts going through my head. I found myself at night laying in my bed and wondering what this is. I would try to blank it out of my mind, but I couldn't. I would even try to walk pass the mirror when I got out the tub just so I would not notice it. No one knew the inner pain. No one knew the thoughts that continued to play in my head. No one knew how I felt. On the inside, I wanted to die. I wasn't thinking about anything else but how ugly I was. I just wanted to crawl into a hole and never come out. One night, I got out the tub, and as I walked pass the mirror in the bathroom, I couldn't help but noticed a patch on my elbow. It was big. Then I looked at my other elbow and noticed a smaller patch. For so long, I tried to blank it out of my mind so much so that I didn't notice how my skin pigment was rapidly changing. So, a moment can be just that a moment, or it can be life changing, and life altering moment. At one point in my life I wish I never had to face

THE DARK SIDE THAT BIRTHED MY WORSHIP

that moment but as God has shown me it was necessary. The Journey begins.

CHAPTER 2
BACK TO SCHOOL (NEW LOOK)

It was the summer of 1990. It was towards the end of the summer to be exact, and the way it started for me was not the way it ended. It was time for me to go back to school. I was entering in to the seventh grade. I was so scared, but I kept it to myself. I was afraid of what people might think of me. I was not ready to explain what I really didn't know what to explain. Meaning I didn't know what was happening to my skin so I didn't have an answer to all the questions. I went to the neighborhood school, so I knew most of the students because they were from the same neighborhood. You would think I would be excited to go back to school like most kids on their first day of school, but I wasn't. I remember when I was in the sixth grade, all we would do is talk about what color of backpack we would be getting for the next grade. What sport I would play etc. This was a big year for me because I was about to enter middle school. I should have been excited, but I wasn't completely. A small part of me was excited, but deep down, I was terrified. I painted the picture of excitement to my parents, friends and those around me. My cousins and I would talk about what we were going to do in the coming year. What sport we would play and so on. Even as I

THE DARK SIDE THAT BIRTHED MY WORSHIP

write this, I can feel the overwhelmed flutters in my stomach. I was so afraid to go to school because I had to face the looks from the kids. Not my friends but from those who hadn't seen me all summer, those who were anticipating reuniting with me for the new school year. I was afraid to face them. I was afraid to face those who would walk pass me in the hallways. I was afraid to face those teachers and mothers and fathers that would pull their children to the side to get away from me as if I was an infection. This is what I dreaded. The last week leading up to my first day of school was the worst. I got sick to my stomach. My emotions were so messed up that I was angry and sad at the same time. I remember laying in my bed at night and thought about what I would say if someone asked me about my skin. I would play it in my head over and over what I would do if someone asked. In those moments, I would get so angry at God. I would look up to the ceiling and ask God, "Why? Why me? Why did I have to be the one to change? Why God? What did I do to deserve this?" I was in that bed sinking and I wanted to do just that, sink. Now, you may be wondering to yourself, "It's just your skin." You probably are wondering what the big deal is. Well, to you it wouldn't be a big deal. You were not the one who had to look in the mirror every day and see your appearance change before you. Not only have that but imagine you being a little girl with no emotional support. No one could explain or tried to explain what was happening. All you would get is, "You are alright." Laying in the bed sick to my stomach, I began to scratch the patches on my fingers. I would scratch so hard until it was burning and bleeding. I was so numb to the pain though. I didn't notice I was scratching myself so hard I was breaking my skin. I guess I thought if I could rub and scratch hard enough, my skin would come back. This was my dark side. This was the time when the enemy would take over my mind. I didn't know what I was doing or what was happening to me. In my mind, this was my way of expressing myself without being shut down or ignored. No one saw my tears or my pain. I could cry out and no one would hear me. I could complain, and no one would hear. It was in that moment no one would be staring at me or whispering around me. Sometimes I wondered how my brothers felt; if they felt anything at all when it came to me and what I was dealing with. Again, we never talked about our feelings in the household I lived in. I never heard them talk to my parents about it, but I'm sure they did. I'm sure they had questions and I'm sure they were protecting my feelings, but I wished they still asked. Maybe this would allow me to not carry this inner pain. The patches

THE DARK SIDE THAT BIRTHED MY WORSHIP

began to spread while the darkness began to grow. By the end of the summer, my face, arms, and knees were affected by this disorder. I was a different little girl on the outside. It seemed like time was not on my side. Not only did I look different on the outside, but my attitude was also different. I felt this inner offense manifesting inside and it wasn't good. I didn't realize the change in my attitude at first but when I started seventh grade is when it became noticeable especially the way I interacted with others around me. In the summer, I tried so hard to act normal with my friends. When I say normal, I mean in the sense of acting like nothing was wrong with me. My skin is fine, and nothing was changing is what I wanted to believe. That's the way I acted and carried myself. I didn't want to look like the kid with the issue. I went so far as trying to prove myself and trying to be the best at whatever I did. When we played, I would try to make sure I could do whatever my peers were doing and try to do it better? I didn't want to be the pity case.

    The morning of the first day of school came. As I opened my eyes, I began to look up to the ceiling and the thoughts began to flood my mind. While all the butterflies were rapidly moving in my stomach, I was trying to decide on how I could make myself sick so that I didn't have to go to school. It took me a minute, finally I said to myself, "Toya you have to face this, so you might as well get up and get this day over with." I got up, went to the bathroom, and got dressed. I was cute for my first day, but I felt completely horrible on the inside. I walked out the house and ran down the street to catch up with my friends who were ahead of me, and here come the stares as soon as we turn the corner. You know kids can be so cruel in their own curious way. When you think about it, kids really don't understand, but you do have some that are just completely cruel. Some kids just don't have a filter. As I got closer to the school, the more stares I got. And then it began. This kid comes to me out of nowhere stop me right in my track and asks, "What happened to your face?" I kept walking and then I hear him say, "She looked like a raccoon by the eyes." I heard it, but I just kept on walking with my head down like I heard nothing. When I made it to class, there was this kid who didn't hold back anything. I couldn't get to me seat good enough before he started with the questions. He asked had what happened to me. I ignored him at first. We were seated in class, and he was sitting in front of me. He turned around and was so loud and rude. He shouted out so loud, "Girl what the hell happened to you?" I felt so embarrassed. At that

THE DARK SIDE THAT BIRTHED MY WORSHIP

moment, I was put on the spot. The class was completely silent, and all eyes were on me. While feeling embarrassed, I also felt this level of rage rising in me from the pit of my stomach. This level of anger and guardedness came over me, and I looked at him for a long time. Then I responded and said, "I was on crack, and the pipe blew up in my face." As crazy as that sounds, that was the first thing that came to my mind. He was so rude and loud, so I decided to take that moment and take the focus off me because I was so embarrassed. The entire class started laughing. He looked at me and started laughing, telling me I was crazy and kept asking what happened. After joking about it he left it alone. I never told him what happened. I just deflected the energy off me and kept it on him. After that, it seemed as if I had this shield up and was ready whenever someone would say something concerning my pigment or would sit and stare. I had this defense up, and my response to people depended on who approached me. So, what I decided was to ask the same question to whoever asked me. After I made the crack pipe joke, and everyone was laughing, I turned and asked him what happened to him. Then he realized how bothered I felt with his questions and how upset I started to get, he finally turned around in his seat and didn't say anything else. See by this time the patches were too big to hide. So, it was nothing I could do to hide or avoid the stares and questions. I got so tired trying to hide my face by looking down knowing that conversations were going on around me. I never held my head up unless someone was asking me a question, or the teacher was teaching other than that I kept my head down all the time. When I changed classes, I would look towards the wall unless someone I knew from the neighborhood would get my attention. By midday, I got so overwhelmed I asked my teacher if I could go to the washroom. Once I got there, I went into the stall and just buried my face between my legs and cried. I was sitting there trying to accept that this was my life now, and this is what I would have to deal with for the rest of my life. I was holding in so much in those few hours, and in a moment, I felt I couldn't take it anymore. I had to let these emotions out. I tried so hard to smile and make the jokes to keep others laughing but also to keep me from breaking down right before them. I finally wiped my face and went back to class. Most of the day had passed, and now it was lunchtime. The lunchroom was another experience in itself. At this point, I realized that I would not only see my classmates, but all the other students in the school as well. These kids I've seen many times, but none I had seen over the summer. I

THE DARK SIDE THAT BIRTHED MY WORSHIP

felt like I was walking the green mile going into the lunchroom with my class. While in the washroom, I coached myself on how I would respond to questions for the rest of the day. I thought I had gotten pass the painful part, but here I am again. As I stood in line, a girl behind me asked a question, "Are you okay?" Initially, I was defensive; I looked at her and asked her why. She was so shocked at how I responded, she just walked away. I felt bad because I knew I was so harsh towards her. I tried to look for her once I got my lunch, but I never did find her. I felt horrible inside, and all I kept thinking was, "If I had just said nothing, I maybe could have had a new friend." She might have been just as scared as I was on her first day. I was so ready to defend myself if someone asked me about the way I looked that I didn't consider others. While sitting at the lunch table, a little boy comes to sit next to me and realized I was the same person from last year and then he remembered my name. He sat next to me and began talking. Asking me questions about my summer vacation. He talked with me as if he didn't notice the patches on my face or hands. I felt like the one time someone sees me for me. I mean someone other than my friend's. Eventually, we became the best of friends. I did have other friends in elementary school, but this was a close friendship. My lunch for the first day turned out to be good. I made it through the first day of school, besides the moments I had. Walking home from school, I did have my neighborhood friends to walk with. Afterwards, me and my friends laughed about the antics of the day which for a moment, made me numb to the reality of my darkness. I was always grateful for the close friends I did have. They never once asked about my skin. I often wondered why. I would say little things about my skin, but they would brush it off it as if it was nothing. There were those who claim to be my friends in the neighborhood that I grew up with but really wasn't. I would often hear conversations and whisper about how ugly I looked and why they don't invite me to their house or to hang out with them. This was one of the many things I hated: the whispers and walking up on kids and everyone getting quiet or walking away making it obvious they were just having a conversation about me. Girls, from the next block covering their mouths while talking, whispering, and snickering. Sometimes when I walk home from school alone, I would run into one of those same kids that was just talking or making fun about me walking alone to. I wouldn't say anything but the way they would act approaching me would make it obvious they were phony. Sometimes I would pray to see someone I knew walking in my direction so I could walk with

THE DARK SIDE THAT BIRTHED MY WORSHIP

them just so I wouldn't have to deal with it. When I got home most days, I would go into my room and laid in my bed burying myself under my covers. I believe a part of me wished my mother would have come in and ask how my day went. But no one came in. At times, I believed I wasn't noticed at all. No one was concerned or showed any concern about what I dealt with on my first day and the days after, although I wasn't surprised. As I stated before, we didn't talk or express our feelings in our home, so it should not have bothered me, but a small part of me still felt bothered.

CHAPTER 3
NOW I KNOW

The first day of going back to school was behind me. I survived to say the least. Oftentimes, I would have to put a kid back in their place or stop someone from walking up to me staring in my face, but for the most part I was surviving by making others see me as a joke. To divert the attention from me, I continued to make jokes about my skin and why I looked the way I did. To be honest, I never knew at that time why my skin was changing. My parents had not taken me to a doctor yet. At this point, I still had no clue what was going on with me or what was the cause of my pigment change. Remember I was told it would go away as if it wasn't a big deal. I was told that the same thing happened to my mother due to a horrific accident. The only difference was that her pigment turned dark. Well, while hers went away, mine didn't. By this time, the patches had grown and become more and more visible. As time went on, my parents decided to take me to the doctor. We went to the University of Chicago. I remember sitting in the waiting room. My mind was going in circles not knowing what to expect. There I sat, my hands sweating, legs shaking and wanting to cry. I went into the room with the doctor, and he looked upon my face and skin.

THE DARK SIDE THAT BIRTHED MY WORSHIP

While he was looking at me and trying to figure me out, I was looking at him and trying to figure him out. My parents were quiet and probably wondering what was on his mind like I was. While he examined me, he asked several questions. I remember him asking my parents if I was allergic to foods, if I had anemia, if I had any surgeries since birth. I'm thinking to myself, "What does that have to do with my skin changing its color." Now a part of me felt relieved because we would finally know what was happening to me. Another part of me was confused because I wondered why it took so long for my parents to bring me to the doctor. I was experiencing so many emotions at the time. I wondered for a long time, if they would have brought me earlier, could I have been treated and maybe cured. If I knew earlier, I could have avoided the made-up stories to divert the unknown. I'm supposed to be thinking about jumping rope and swinging on the swings in the park. Instead, here I am at the age of twelve wondering what is happening to my life. I never was a bold kid. I was very sensitive, and I cried all the time. When I say cry all the time, I mean I found myself crying explaining myself. While sitting in the doctor's room, I remember my dad asking me how I felt, and I started crying. We sat waiting for the doctor to come back with the results of my tests.

The doctor came back and began to tell my parents and me the report. He told us that I was suffering from an autoimmune disorder called Vitiligo.

Vitiligo (vit-ill-EYE-go) is a disorder in which white patches of skin appear on different parts of the body.

This happens because the cells that make pigment (color) in the skin are destroyed. These cells are called **melanocytes (ma-LAN-o-sites).** *Vitiligo can also affect the mucous membranes such as the tissue inside the mouth and nose and the eye.* The doctor also told me that I was anemic which is a red blood cell deficiency. I had no clue what the doctor was talking about, and I don't think my parents did either at that time. It was so confusing to me. The more he talked and tried to explain, the more confused I was. The doctor began to ask my parents a series of questions. He asked about our family history. If there was anyone from prior generations affected by this disorder. I thought to myself, "Why am I here?" I felt like I was in a Charlie Brown episode. What is happening to me? I was hurting on the inside all while the doctor is talking. Thinking to myself, all I wanted to do is go home. The last thing I remember the doctor telling my parents is that there was no cure. He said there was no cure, only treatment. He said that I could

THE DARK SIDE THAT BIRTHED MY WORSHIP

only take treatments which would slow down the progression of the disorder. He told them all the medical things that were happening with my cells and how the melanocytes were being destroyed. All while he was talking, I could feel my body drifting away. I wanted to crawl out the window while my parents sat there and listened to the doctor. I know he was doing his job and I believe he thought he had my best interest at heart. But for me, I wanted to disappear. The doctor began to tell my parents the things I needed to do as a form of treatment. I was to take all these different vitamins; one for iron, one for the anemia, another for low vitamin D, and Vitamin A. I was to eat a lot of vegetables–green vegetables. He also told my parents and me that I needed to eat food that are high in iron. I must eat large portions of liver or lean meats, blah blah blah. Among other things, I had to take cod liver oil every day. This would give me enough antitoxins to slow down my melanin destruction. I remember him saying nothing ultimately can be done to stop the changing of my pigment, only to slow it down. I remember he said that this is not an area that much research had been done on. Then I wondered, "What's the point? Why am I here?" He mentioned I would have to drink a lot of water and increase my mineral intake as well. My iron was low, so the intake needed to be very high. The doctor also told my parents that I would have to go through radiation treatment at least twice a week along with the medication to slow down the discoloration of my pigment or reverse it. Again, I felt like I was in a Charlie Brown episode. I thought to myself, "There is no cure, so why are we still here?" It felt like my life was being sucked right out of me. What the doctor did not talk about was the emotional and physiological effect this could have on a child. I felt sick by the time we left the doctor's office. I was overwhelmed with emotions; I was hurt, angry, disappointed, and confused. My heart was torn. I just wanted to vanish. My dad asked me how I felt, and I told him I was fine. My mother never said anything. She didn't console me either. My dad grabbed and held me; he told me everything was going to be okay. Even though he said that, I knew deep down inside that it wasn't. I knew he was telling me that to make me feel better. I don't think anyone of us knew exactly how to express our feelings, to be honest. This was all new to all of us, so I'm sure it was hard for my parents to deal with, but still, no one could ever walk in my shoes. We got home from the hospital, and we never talked about it again. That night alone in my room, I sat there, and the only thing that kept playing in my mind was that there is no cure. Nothing could

THE DARK SIDE THAT BIRTHED MY WORSHIP

be done to reverse this disorder. This played in my head over and over. I was in complete disbelief. There is no cure!! There is no cure!!! While this is playing in my head, I could feel my arms getting hot. I began scratching the patches so hard it felt like I was burning myself with a lighter. I laid in my bed, face in the pillows and would not move. I began to feel the breath fade out of my chest, but I didn't get up. I stayed there, slowly trying to suffocate myself. This voice was saying in my ear, "There is no cure, why live?" I felt myself sinking deeper and deeper and all of a sudden, I felt something pull me up as if someone else was in the room. I know that sounds crazy, but that's what happened. Next thing I know, I was kneeling on the side of my bed in a pool of tears. I laid there in a pool of tears asking the question WHY until I fell asleep right on the edge of my bed. Days after that my mom would make me liver and I would be forced to eat it. I began to take vitamins and eating more and more green vegetables. I never went back to the doctor again until I became a young adult. We never looked into other options nor did my parents seek to get me some type of help or counseling on how to deal with the emotional toll this eventually took on me.

CHAPTER 4
MY SAFE HAVEN

One of the things I did was try to keep myself busy in and out of school. I kept myself engaged in various activities. I was a part of a youth program that allowed us to work over the summer at the school we attended. I tried to keep myself busy and stay involved with different programs in the school just to keep my mind at ease and not be bothered about what was going on with my skin. As another summer drew nearer, it never crossed my mind that this was the last year at this school and that I would be going to high school. I survived seventh grade, and I felt that the eighth grade wouldn't be as cruel, seeing that everyone now knows about the skin disease that had invaded my body. The shock was over, and I was the girl with the spots. People had given me nicknames of all sorts. You would be in complete shock as to some of the things I was called during this time. I guess the one that was insane enough to stick was "spots." I was the girl with the spots. I was often reminded of the 101 Dalmatians Disney movies by several students at my school. In case you don't know, the 101 Dalmatians were white puppies with black spots all over their bodies. People would

THE DARK SIDE THAT BIRTHED MY WORSHIP

still ask me, "What happened?" And I would make up something right on the spot, or I would tell the truth. Those who were very rude would get the sarcasm, but to those who were just curious, I would give them a soft response. Besides dealing with the cruelty of the kids, I often had to deal with the ignorance of the parents. I will never forget a day on the bus. As I was sitting, a mother and her daughter came in and sat next to me. The mother initially didn't look up, but the daughter did. She was a little girl no more than three or four years old. She pointed at my face and said, "Mommy, what's the matter with her?" Her mother looked over at me and gave this disgusting look. She grabbed her daughter and told her to get away from me. I felt the tears forming in my eyes, and I held my head down. They got up and moved to another area on the bus. From that day on, I never sat towards the back of the bus, I would only sit right in the front. Imagine the pain I felt. People sitting there looking at me as if I did something wrong. The bus driver turned and said, some people are just plain ignorant. One of the other things I loved to do while growing up, was go to the church. I grew up in our family home church. This I can say was the one of a couple of places I called my safe haven. My fondest memories are of the church and growing up around my friends that are like family. The church was the place I felt I could escape the ugliness of the world around me. I was a part of the youth church, that I was a part of since I was a little girl. No one bothered me when it came to my skin in the church. Either the children there were too afraid to ask me directly, or they would ask their parents. Most of the kids in the church I grew up in were family, so I didn't have to do a lot of explaining, as they kind of watched me grow through the process. There were times I would get treated some type of way but not as often. Here I found myself not having to hide my face. I mean I didn't have to make up stories, and I didn't have to be silent and feel ashamed to speak. But in school, as I stated before, there were good and bad days. It was cool not having to explain myself or end up saying some sarcastic or smart remarks around my church family. Sometimes I would say something that would point to my patches, and they would look at me clueless as if they didn't know what I was saying. Many would tell me they don't notice the patches and that I looked fine. I believe this was a way for the little girl to cry out and talk about her true feelings and let what she was feeling come out. During this time, I grew more as a Christian, and I was getting more involved with the youth church. The youth pastor took a lot of the youth as his own children. He treated us with much love and was so fun to be around. He made learning about God so much fun and interesting that I was always hungry to know more. I remember the days when he would come to pick us up from the house on weekends so we could come to church for rehearsal. He made sure we were there. He became a spiritual father to me as well as many others. One day I didn't have a good night, and I felt bothered the next morning. All I wanted to do was go to church, but my mother gave me so much hell trying to stop me from going. This was because she had been up all night long partying and usually when that happens, I would be the target that she would pick fights with all night long. My mother had demons that she dealt with in her own way. I believe one of those was how she treated me. Again, the only girl and middle child but for some reason, I felt I was the one she hated most. It seemed like this type of treatment that I endured growing up started happening after I began to go through the changes with my skin. My grandmother lived in the same building as we did, and her place was my second safe haven. Those nights and weekends when my mother would be wrestling with her demons, I would run to my granny's house until it was safe to go back home. This night was one of those nights I couldn't escape to my granny's house and let time pass until it was safe to go back home to my room and sleep. It was one of those nights I had to endure the yelling and arguing. It was never because I did anything wrong; it was because I was there in her presence. Alcohol was a big factor in our house, and I was the one that would be there to catch the bad end of it. This morning, it was time to get up to church. I was already running late, and I had missed my ride with my granny, so I called the Rev. Luckily, I caught him just in time. I was so sad when I got in the van. He looked at me in the rear-view mirror and said, "What's wrong with you?" I answered him with a vague response. He began driving and chewing gum. Rev had a way of getting you to talk to him. He would pull his glasses down on his nose and then ask you, "Who do you think you are talking to? I know you." So, he asked me again, "What's the problem?" Again, I replied, "I'm okay." He gave me this look as if he could read right through my mind. I began to break down and then he told me we would talk about it later. Before the service was over, he pulled me to the side and said, "Now what was your problem this morning?" I began to tell him I had noticed another spot growing on my body. I told him that when I told my mother about it the night before, she began to use some very harsh words and made me feel like it wasn't that big of a deal to her. She told

THE DARK SIDE THAT BIRTHED MY WORSHIP

me to get over it and get used to the fact that I was changing. She was so cutthroat that I felt it pierce my chest and go straight to my heart. The problem was when I told her this, I didn't realize it would come back to haunt me after she began drinking. When that happened, she came back to me as if she wanted to talk about it, but it ended up in her attacking me verbally. I told him that I didn't get much sleep and that's why I was bothered. And when I got up to get ready for church, she came into the room again and was saying things as to why I was going to church. Being a little girl even then, I learned how to deal with the verbal abuse the best way I could. He just listened to me as I was telling him what had happened in detail. He then turned to me and asked me how it made me feel, and why does that bother me so much. I asked him what he meant by that. He asked me if my skin changing bothered me and if it did, why did it bother me so much. I gave him the craziest look and said, "Rev, look at me, I'm turning into a white girl." He laughed so hard at me. It was the funniest thing to him. I was serious, and he was laughing. He kept laughing until I started laughing and my tears became tears of laughter and not pain anymore. Once he stopped laughing, he then reached out to hug me and told me, "God made you this way. When you get older, you will understand that you are special to Him and He needs you for a reason to go through this process, so when the time comes, you will change the life of someone else." I said, "Why me though?" He said, "Why not you? You are His special and the chosen one." He continued by saying, "You had to be the one He used so you can tell other girls how beautiful they are because He showed you how beautiful you are." I began to smile, and at that moment, I felt at ease. All the tears and pain I endured that night till morning did not matter at that moment. He then told me to talk with his wife, Mrs. Rev. He also mentioned that she had something to give me. We never talked about the incident anymore, at that point, it didn't matter much anymore. When I got to church that following week, I found his wife, and she sat with me and began to ask me questions about how I was feeling. She asked me how I was dealing with this whole process of my skin changing. Then she asked me how I was sleeping at night. At first, I didn't understand the question, so she rephrased the question. She asked, "Was I getting any sleep or was I up thinking about how I would be able to live with this disorder?" It was like she knew something was going on with me. I told her I was fine, and she smiled and said, "When you're ready to talk about it, you will." She gave me some instructions: she told me that every

THE DARK SIDE THAT BIRTHED MY WORSHIP

morning before I get ready for school, I should get on my knees and say this prayer. She gave me a prayer specifically for my skin.

Prayer for my skin.

Thank you, God, for making me the way I am, you love me so much you made me special. Today I claim my healing. My skin and my life are normal I am who you say I am and that's all that matter's

I love you God.

At first, I didn't understand because she told me to say it every single morning before I went to school. I wondered why I should do the same thing every day. Before I could say anything, she told me that until God hears my prayer, I need to keep declaring my healing. The last thing she did was give me this Cod Liver Oil to take. She told me to take a tablespoon every day. It was to help with the patches and my skin. It was supposed to reverse the progression of the patches. I came home and told my mother what happened and what Mrs. Rev said. And she told me, "Okay, let's try it and see if it works." From what it seemed; she had already talked to Mrs. Rev about it. That was good because then I wouldn't have to hide it or feel like she wouldn't understand. Besides the church. I join the Majorette team at my school. I believe I was one of the best on the team. Unfortunately, I couldn't stay on the team because of what was going on at home. I had no support, and I had no one that would make sure I was able to travel with the team. When it came to the shows, no one was there, and I had no way of getting to the school and getting back home. So eventually, I had to get off the team. This was a devastating moment in my youth because I was so happy and good at it, and for the first time, I felt like I was needed. It didn't matter about what I looked like; I was accepted for what I did. They tried what they could to keep me on the team, and the coach did so much, but it just couldn't happen. I was hurt and broken because the one thing I was good at was taken away from me without an explanation. I also wanted this because it helped shift my focus from my skin to something I loved.

CHAPTER 5
THE MAKE UP

Eighth grade was going well for me. I was thirteen years old a preteen. By this time, everyone was used to the girl with the patches. Often, I would have to encounter a kid that would say something ignorant, but for the most part, I could say bullying was not an issue in elementary school. Now that it is getting close to the end of the school year, my luncheon and graduation dance were two big things that I had to face. All the girls were

talking about it. It was an exciting time for everyone. On one hand, I wanted to go, and on the other, I didn't. I wanted to go and enjoy being a girly girl with nothing but fun and laughter. But the inner little girl wanted to stay in her dark space and sit and talk about all the reason she didn't want to be seen. The little girl within wanted to be alone. She tried to convince me that I was not pretty enough and that I wasn't going to look half as pretty as the other girls. So, she tried to convince me not to go. The other side of me wanted to go and enjoy the dance with my friends. Now, my friends, they had young boyfriends they wanted to go to the dance with. I didn't. At this point, I never liked anyone, and I don't think anyone liked me. We didn't have a school dance, but another school had one, and my friends planned to go there. This dance was in a couple of weeks, and I had not made up my mind if I was going to go or not. Finally decided to go and no matter what, enjoy myself with my friends. My friends and I planned to wear the same outfits. As I said before, the patches had spread in other areas of my body. It was beginning to grow more rapidly again. The patches that were already visible were spreading wider.

One day, my dad came home and began to tell me about this cream. He tells me about a lady at his job who told him about this cream that specializes in matching your skin tone. The name of the cream was called Fashion Fair. He told me that this cream would match my skin tone perfectly. He said I could cover up the spots and not have to worry about the way I looked in the public. I was pretty excited and curious at the same time. I did play with my cousins a little with makeup but nothing beyond wearing lip gloss. So, this was something new. It's funny because my dad was the one that took me shopping for clothes and whatever else I needed growing up. Now he's taking me to go shopping for makeup. He was the one that showed me how to get on the bus in the city. He took me to get my job permit to work when I was fourteen. My mother never did any of those things with me, she was more

THE DARK SIDE THAT BIRTHED MY WORSHIP

reserved. Those things little girls look to do with their mothers, I didn't experience those things with her only my dad. Spending that mother and daughter time was never something we did. Getting back to the cream, after we talked about this cream, I was more and more curious of what it looks like, how I would look with it on, and would it make my skin look normal. I would never stop using it. I had already pictured myself in the makeup.

I pictured all the pain, hurt, and anger gone away. I pictured my life going back to normal. It took me back to that day I noticed a spot on my right index finger. I imagine it being normal no more spots. Days went by, and I decided to tell my parents I wanted to try it. The weekend came, and my parents were off work. We got

up and took the bus to downtown Chicago. Now this was an over the counter makeup cream; something that you would use to even your skin tone and cover the blotches that sometimes appear in the face of women. The day comes for us to go I was holding back every emotion I could. We finally got off the bus, and immediately, I can feel the knots in my stomach. I felt like a little person in a big world. It seemed like all the people around me were giants, and I was this little girl. There goes that feeling again of me feeling like I was sinking into a black hole. We got to the counter, and I could hear my parents explaining to the lady what my condition was and about this cream that could cover the patches. She turns to me and tells me to sit in the highchair. She turned me away from the mirrors and began to ask me how I felt. I told her I was okay. She then explains to me about the cream. She begins to tell me step by step what she was going to be doing to my face. She was a very nice lady, and she took her time. She told me to relax. Now, we were at Carson's—which was one of the world's biggest stores—in downtown Chicago. It was a Saturday, so imagine how busy this store was. So many people from different cultures stopping and slowing down as they walk past me gazing at my face. I closed my eyes and began to sing that song I hear all the time at church: "God has smiled on me; He has set me free." I had my eyes closed for a while because I didn't want to see the people staring at me. Time had passed, and it seemed like she was taking forever, but she finally finished. I didn't open my eyes right away. I was so nervous of what I might look like. The other part of my brain was telling me to get up and open my eyes. I just couldn't move; I was too nervous. You would think I would be super excited because I finally would be able to have a normal child life, but I was scared to death. She finally asked if I was ready and then turned me around to the

THE DARK SIDE THAT BIRTHED MY WORSHIP

mirror. I finally opened my eyes and looked in the mirror. I looked for a long time. And then I turned to my dad and told him I didn't like it and that I wanted to go home. I could feel the tears forming. The lady looked and asked, "What's wrong?" I told her to take it off I don't like it. Then I put my head down. I looked up at the mirror again, my lips and hands shaking. It wasn't that she did something wrong and it wasn't that it didn't blend, or it looked bad, but when I looked in the mirror, I saw a face covered up entirely with this makeup. I felt like I had a mask put over my face. I was more embarrassed with the makeup on than with it off. I felt more ashamed of how I looked instead of feeling better. It was so perfect, yet so imperfect. I believe that in that moment, God was showing me that I was covering up the beauty He created me to be. I believe this is God showing how we as people, put on this entire mask to give the appearance of something perfect, but the real look is the imperfection that shows. My mom told me to just wear it for that day and see how I feel then. She thought maybe I would change my mind. I didn't, I wanted the lady to take it off my face right then and there. I looked at my dad and told him I don't want it for a second time, and he looked at me and said, "Babe, you don't have to wear if you don't want to." He politely told the lady to take it off. We left and got back on the bus, and all I did was look out the window. On the way home, I was trying to figure out why I didn't want to wear something that would cover the patches. I wanted the patches gone. This was my constant prayer to take this horrible defect away from me. I didn't ask for it and I didn't want it. So why didn't I want the make up? The very thing that would cover up the ugliness I hate to look at every day. I couldn't figure it out. While riding home looking out the window tears began to flow. We oftentimes want to cover up the imperfections that in God's eyes, are perfect. I prayed for them to be gone and out of my life. I prayed for my life to go back to the way it was before this. When we got back around the house I went straight to my friend's house, and I told her what had happened. I showed her the sample the lady in the store gave me to keep in case I changed my mind. I showed my friend Quita the makeup and she went off. She asked me what I need it for, and I told her what it could do. She laughed so hard but at the same got so mad. For some reason, she was mad I would even consider covering up my skin. How confusing is that! Well, to this day, the question remains unanswered. All I can tell you is that I felt horrible with the cream on. Now as an adult and someone who has grown in God, I understand that God made me this way and to cover that

THE DARK SIDE THAT BIRTHED MY WORSHIP

up would be covering up Him. Now I understand, I was chosen to be the person in my family to experience this. Now I understand, if I wore the makeup, that would make me one who would cover up all the imperfections and no room to be made perfect. When I finally got home, I went to the bathroom and looked in the mirror, and the tears wouldn't stop. I looked at this little raccoon face and felt relieved. I told myself right in that mirror, "God has smiled on me. He has set me free." I cried and yet smiled. I thought I wanted to cover up the patches and this would make me free. But in reality, it would have only put me in more bondage. When I came out the bathroom, my dad hugged me. He told me I never have to wear that cream again and that I was beautiful just the way I am. The lady at the store did show me how to put it on. She gave me all the instructions on how to care for my skin. I believe this was the turning point for me. I believe this was the point I realized that, this is who I am. I can't describe the feeling, but it was something to remember. Sometimes out of fear, we want to cover up the very thing God is trying to highlight in our lives. We look at it as being ugly, imperfect, wrong, too small, etcetera. So, we use all our power and might to cover it up. This is the very thing God wants to highlight in us, through us and around us. He wants to make sure you know that He has chosen the defective and most painful parts of our lives to get the glory out of it. Of course, at thirteen, I didn't know or had even thought to care about that.

CHAPTER 6
THE DANCE

It was the night of the eighth-grade dance. Up unto this point, I was beginning to feel more confident about myself. I didn't have the longest hair and the prettiest body and no, I didn't know how to wear makeup, but I did take what I had to wear and thought I looked like a million dollars in spite of what my skin looked like. In my neighborhood, fortunately I was not treated as an outcast in spite of because we all had one thing in common, we lived in the HOOD. This night, the weather was perfect. No rain and no cold weather. The dance was at another school, so I barely knew anyone there except my close friends I was going with. The hour came for me to get dressed. After getting out of the shower and pulling out my outfit, finishing up my hair, I go into the bathroom and pulled out the cream. Remember the cream that I despised. Well, I never threw the sample the consultant at Carson's had given me away. I pulled the cream out and sat it on the bathroom sink. I looked in the mirror to see my face, and for a moment, I stared at the cream. I was fully dressed, but for some reason I needed to cover my face. I was getting ready by myself so no one could talk me out of it. So, the only opinion I had was the one of myself. I began to remember what the consultant showed me on how to apply the cream. I never picked up the cream after I showed my best friend, so I was a little nervous. It was my first time applying it. I began to put the cream on my face. I tried to remember the way the lady did it and follow her steps. Once I finished, I looked up, and to my surprise, it blended well. I didn't have that feeling I had when she put it on my face in the store. Although while I was putting it on, I was shaking with fear and anxiety. I didn't see any blemishes. In my eyes, it blended well, and it was even. For one night, I just wanted to be looked at for me and not because of my skin. I wanted to be looked at and being asked to dance because I was beautiful not because I was pitied. You could still see the patches but only if you were close to my face. The rest of my body was covered. I did however, put a little cream on some areas on my legs so they didn't look so white. After putting on the cream and looking at myself in the mirror, I can say I felt pretty on the inside and out. I came out of the bathroom, and I hurried and grabbed my jacket and left. We got on the bus to go to the party. I was so self-conscious about the makeup that, I found myself on the bus looking around to see who was staring in my face. My friends never said a word. They just told me how pretty I looked and that they were happy I came outside with them. We

THE DARK SIDE THAT BIRTHED MY WORSHIP

got to the place, and there were a lot of kids there. The party was for thirteen to eighteen-year old. The gym was dark, and you really couldn't see anyone unless you were up close. Everything seemed to be going well. We were having some much fun. I got to meet new people. We were dancing and having a good time. Found myself dancing with this guy that seemed to be into me. The next thing I know, we were around each other all night. We were having so much fun. For the first time I felt free. I felt normal with no worries. I wasn't a shame or isolated. In that moment I didn't feel the stress of being accepted. The focus was not on what was on my face but me. I was smiling, laughing and dancing having so much fun. Then it happened. The moment of what was once a perfect night turned into a complete nightmare. The dance had come to an end. The lights came on, and it was time to go. I was having so much fun that I got disconnected from my friends. Everyone was rushing towards the exit door some kind of way I got disconnected from the guy I was with most of the night as well. I couldn't see him in the crowd anymore. My friends could not be located. We were all separated. I ended up in the hallway by the exit door. Next thing I know someone walk up to me asking what was wrong with me. I turned and look up; it was the guy. The one I had been hanging with the whole night. It was like he was looking at a complete stranger. I said, "Nothing, what are you talking about?" He said, "What is that on your face? You got spots all in your face." I asked him what he was talking about as if I didn't know what he was referring to. He asked me again while his friends walked up to us. Now they are looking at me too and making faces and jokes about my skin. I was speechless at this point. "I didn't see that in your face a minute ago. What happened to you?" The boy continued asking what was wrong with this disgusting look on his face. He backed up from me and said he had to go. We were in the crowd holding hands, next thing I know, I'm sitting by the door trying to see if my friends would walk pass so I could go home. I started to feel horrible and confused. Everyone who walked pass me was either staring or whispering. I could see them pointing and then turning away. The guy was no were to be found, and I was alone sitting in the hallway. I was sinking back into this hole. What started to be one of the most memorable times of my pre-teenage years ended in a nightmare. I got up and went to the bathroom. I wanted to see if I looked as disgusting as the people were looking and treating me. I looked in the mirror, and I noticed the cream had faded on one side and completely gone on the other side, you could see the patches very

THE DARK SIDE THAT BIRTHED MY WORSHIP

clearly. Right there, I wanted to die. I wanted to die right in that moment. I felt like I was part of a movie where the truth was being revealed in a scene, and all eyes were on me. Here I am, in a place I am not familiar with, and my friends are nowhere to be found. I went into a stall, buried my face in my arms and started screaming, but then I realized I still had some of the cream on, so I had to keep it together so I don't mess my clothes up. Finally, I got myself together and went back into the hallway, I ran into one of my friends and not long after, I found the other. They saw the look on my face and ask what happened. I told them "You left me that's what happened." I told them I just wanted to go home. My friend's mom was there to pick us up by this time. Just as we were walking out the door. I see the guy and his friends pointing at me while taunting him. I put my head down and tears began to flow. We got in the car, and I sat in the back seat and was silent the entire time. When I got home, I went straight to my room. Grabbed my pajamas and went into the bathroom. I got the cleansing cloths and began to wipe the rest of the cream from my face. Thoughts began to flood my mind. This is why nobody likes you. Now you see what I have been trying to tell you all along. You thought you were going to cover it up, but it turned out to be worse. The more I wiped, the louder this voice got in my head. I kept hearing her telling me to run some water. Telling me to get in the bathtub and lay there for a while and no one will notice. No one will come and look for me. I opened the medicine cabinet and then I heard her tell me to take the razor in the medicine cabinet and take the rest of the dark skin on my body off. Just take the rest of so you can get this over with. After wiping the cream off my face, I ran my bath water. I felt so alone and isolated in this world by myself. I figured if I cut the rest of the black skin from my body, I would be okay to face the world. I would be okay to go on with one tone and not have to deal with the cruelty of this world. These were the thoughts in my mind that I tried to make a reality. While in the bathroom. Before I got into the tub, I stood in the mirror. While standing there I notice another patch has formed. I just wanted this nightmare to be over. I took the towel, covered my mouth and screamed to the top of my lungs. Then I got in the tub. I just laid there in the water looking up. I laid there for a long time and slowly started sinking in the water. I was so numb. The voice in my mind seemed to get louder and louder, and I found myself going down in the water. I was sinking inside and out. I was drowning in my shame, anger, hurt and pain. I figured no one was going to notice if I was gone. No one cared about how I felt. No one pays attention to me anyway. "What does it matter?" I told God in that moment "you did this." Out of all the people in the world you allowed me to be the one who loses her originality. I was so angry I was sinking deeper and deeper under. Suddenly, this picture of me and my dad on the train appeared in my head. We were riding the train. We had so much fun. I remembered seeing in that image a little girl laughing and smiling, so excited. In this picture, I was happy, I was free. In this picture I didn't have any patches. As we were laughing and seemed to be having a joyous time. My Dad reached over to me pull me into his arms and said," I will never let you down, I will always be here through it all." Then I heard this loud sound and I jumped up out of the water. When I sat up in the tub, I looked around trying to make sense of what just happened. I began to think about how I needed to live because it was something, I had to do no matter what. Also, in that moment, I realized that I tried to end my life. Even though I was in that moment of wanting to fade away forever, something in me wouldn't let me. Even as I write about it, I can feel the inner pain of that moment as if it were just yesterday. I feel all the emotions I felt at that time, even right now.

As I came out of the bathroom, I looked around for someone in the house to see who was woke or even knew I was there. I go in my brothers' room and they were doing what boys usually do. I sat at the foot of the bed. The older one looked at me and asked me what was wrong. I said nothing. Then I turned and said I found another spot. He brushed it off like it was nothing. At that point I got up and went to my room. One of the things my granny taught me was to never go to bed before saying your prayers. So, right before I did, I got on my knees and said my prayers. I would always start with Psalms 23. Once I said my prayers, I would then ask God the big question, "WHY ME?". I was so hurt and confused, and I couldn't understand why. I began to ask what is happening to me. It was like I was waiting on God to answer me. I would tell God that this was not supposed to be the life of a little girl. I laid there, and the tears began to flow heavily. It's like, one minute I am fine, and the next minute I would be overwhelmed with anger and emotions. The little girl inside of me wanted to overpower me and cause me to sink and drown in my emotion. Even in those moments I still would find myself singing inwardly. Singing was something I would do when I'm alone. This night was very different. I was pouring out to the point of feeling pain in my stomach. I remember getting up

THE DARK SIDE THAT BIRTHED MY WORSHIP

from a puddle of tears; my pajamas were drenching wet. My little body was so stiff. I got up from the floor and on to my bed and laid there on my back facing the ceiling. I tried so hard to go to close my eyes, but the longer I laid there staring at the ceiling, the more my mind would replay that night in my head. I rolled over to my cassette player and began to play "The battle is not yours" by Yolanda Adams. While lying there and listening to my music, I heard a small voice telling me I am special. It was so clear and loud that I looked up at my door thinking someone was in the room. I laid back down and then I heard, "You are beautiful." Now my eyes are closed, and I began to close them even harder thinking someone was in the room with me. Then I heard these words, "You were chosen. I chose you for this, and I will keep you through it all." I opened my eyes, and no one was there with me. I closed my eyes again, and I hear those exact words again. I opened my eyes, and it was pitch black in my room. Now at this point, I sit up with my back against my headboard. My first thought was that someone was either in my room or by my window. I got up, switched my light on and looked around. Then I turned the lights off and got back in my bed. As I laid back down, suddenly, a cool feeling came over me, and I felt almost like I was floating in the air. That's the only way to describe it. At first, I was so sad and broken and alone, then a piece of calmness came over me. The tears had gone away, and I started to smile. I didn't understand it then, but now I know it was the peace of God coming over me and soothing my pain and hurt. The peace was settling my mind and thoughts. Now I understand the scripture about peace

Philippians 4:7 And the peace of God, which transcends all understanding, will guard your hearts and your minds in Christ Jesus

I continued to play the song by Yolanda Adams, and I was bathing in God's peace. I felt much serenity during this moment and fell asleep. It was almost time for graduation and to keep myself busy I became a part of the school's speech team. In this group we had to learn and recite poetry. I was excited because not only did I feel accepted, but I was good at it. I was so good I was chosen to represent the school in the state competition. I did a poem called "God's Creation" It was the first 6 verses in the first chapter from the book of Genesis. When it got closer to the competition my teacher continued to Encourage me and help me rehearse. It was so much going on at home the only time I had to rehearse was at school. I remember telling my mom about it, but she didn't go with

THE DARK SIDE THAT BIRTHED MY WORSHIP

us to the competition. When we got there and I got off the bus, the other kids from the other school were there as well. I walked in with my teacher holding my head down. It seemed like my hearing was amplified. I heard every whisper, felt every stare. Anxiety was kicking in. I started shaking, hands sweating, and my cheeks was getting hot. This overwhelming feeling of fear came over me. We made our way to the back of the stage. While waiting to go forward I was a nervous wreck. My teacher asked if I was ready and it was like the enemy took my entire voice. I couldn't speak. She asked was I ok when I said yes you could hear the shakiness in my voice. I was terrified to go out there on that stage and perform in front of an entire auditorium of people. Right before it was my turn, I ran to the washroom to get myself together. In my head all I kept hearing was the voices of those kids I walked pass. I looked. In the mirror I looked at myself and tried to convince myself I was going to fail. I had no one there with me for support or encouragement. So, I figure what's the point. I was so afraid to open my mouth and speak in front of all these people. After I finally got it together, I went back out and waited. My teacher came over to me and said to just do what I been doing don't worry about whose watching close my eyes. Got out on stage and I looked out at the audience and no one I knew beside my other classmates were there. Immediately I was sad, but I had to go on. Started off good. Suddenly, my mind went blank. Right there my mind went completely blank. Only had a second to go on. So, I started over and all of a sudden something came over me and it was as if I was in another place and it was just me. I did the poem. When I finish, I opened my eyes and had a standing novation. I ran off the stage in tears. Amazingly enough I won second place. I was so proud of myself in that moment I couldn't believe it. Got back to the school and then home. Although this was big accomplishment for me, it also was the moment were the spirit of fear settle in. I started having anxiety attacks when someone asks me a question in front of others. I never could express myself without crying it was terrible. This was not good, and I didn't know to stop it. As long as I was in the background, I was fine, the moment I felt called out or on the spot I would fall apart. This level of fear and anxiety consumed me for many years.

CHAPTER 7
ONTO A NEW JOURNEY
(HIGH SCHOOL)

I opened my eyes as the sun shone through my window and unto my face. Today was a big day—another milestone in my life. It was the first day of high school. My emotions were all over the place. This milestone was different from my first day in middle school. By this time everyone around me was used to the way I looked. Still another milestone I wasn't ready for. I started to feel the way I did when I was starting middle school but on another level. All those emotions came rushing back to my mind. I worked over the summer, so I interacted with more kids and adults and became more comfortable around people that I didn't know, but there were still those moments that I would have a break down. Even then I learned how to control my emotions a little better. On the first day, as I laid in my bed that morning, I thought to myself, "What will this day bring? What kind of day will I have? What idiot will I have to encounter and what will I say to get them out of my face?" Then suddenly a rush of anxiety took over my entire body. I got nervous and found myself not being able to move. I laid in the bed, stiff as a board. Eventually I was able to move again. I put the cover over my head and buried myself. My school wasn't in walking distance, so I didn't have one of my friends to walk to school with me like I did in elementary school. This time I would have to take the bus. I imagined myself on the bus and people moving away from me or staring directly in my face, then whispering and just being cruel while I laid there under the covers. I hated it, and I hated the feeling. This was becoming one of my worst days all over again the more these thoughts took over my mind. I felt like I was reliving that first day of school in seventh grade all over again. Not only did I have to take public transportation, but I also had to walk to the bus stop. Again, I thought starting seventh grade was the worst. At least when I started seventh grade, I knew the kids because most of us were in the same classes since we were in kindergarten. So, for me then it was them getting use to the new look. Going into high school was a whole different ball game. This opened a different level of fear and anxiety. You expect the kids in elementary school to be cruel because they didn't know any better and they were just kids. I was in complete defense mode when it came to the kids in my classes, and I also diverted a lot of the pain by saying demeaning jokes to cover the pain and keep me from breaking down. High school was completely different. I didn't know

THE DARK SIDE THAT BIRTHED MY WORSHIP

what to expect. The more I allowed these thoughts to consume my mind the more I started sweating, breathing fast, and shaking. My heart felt like it was beating right out of my chest. While this emotion was taking over my mind and body, I found myself fighting. One side telling me it's cool you will fit right in. The other side telling to give it up, no one is going to accept you. You're too ugly, you look like a raccoon face. These are the thoughts that were constantly playing in my mind. Now, this morning me and my mom were the only ones up in the house as I was getting ready to go to school. My mom was up cooking breakfast for my dad. While I'm walking through the house with these thoughts ringing in my head. I was still smiling on the outside. Now, my elder brother was already in high school, and you would think he would give me a pep talk about what to expect. He didn't. For me, it was just my first day of high school in his eyes. Now by this time, I was ready to leave out for school. I had all my stuff ready to walk out the door. Still shaking and scared, but knew I had to go. Went to the kitchen where my mom was, told her I was leaving. Her response was ok. A part of me was looking for encouragement. Honestly, if she would have turned and look at me, she would have seen the look on my face and knew something wasn't right. As I was walking down the block I started wondering if I would be the only person in the entire school that look the way I did. I guess if there was someone that looked like me then I wouldn't feel so alone. I wouldn't feel like the all the attention would be on me. When you look at someone with a disability, people tend to pity them. People are moved by compassion. But for me, I was the person that would be made fun of, not only behind my back but in my face. The looks, stares and being made to feel like I was a disease, is what I was dreading. My mind was racing while I was walking to the bus stop. This little girl was trying to overwhelm me with all these emotions. Suddenly, I heard something within say, "You are not afraid." I heard it again "You are not afraid. "2 Timothy 1:7 (NIV) For the Spirit God gave us does not make us timid, but gives us power, love and self-discipline, came forth out of my mouth. I learned this scripture as a youth, and this is one of many that I still carry in my heart. I repeated this scripture in my mind until I no longer heard the thoughts of the other voice. As I was walking, I just began to sing. Making melodies in my heart unto the Lord is something I would do. I had to figure out a way to keep my mind from sinking so I would sing. While walking to the bus stop, I began to see other kids walking in the same directions. I got to the bus stop, and as I was standing there,

THE DARK SIDE THAT BIRTHED MY WORSHIP

all of a sudden, a car pulled up. It was one of the guys that I knew from my neighborhood. He pulled over and asked me if I wanted to ride to school. He also had his friends with him in the car from the block, so I was comfortable enough to get in. Pulled up to the school and I started feeling this knot form in my stomach. The guys from the block were seniors at the school, and they played basketball, so I was with some of the most popular guys in school. I got out of the car and started walking towards the school. Talk about envy and the look on the other kids' face. They wanted to say something, but they didn't because of who I was with. To this day, I'm not sure if he did that out of pity or just being generous. I didn't have to curse any one out for insulting me or saying something out of pocket as I would have if I was on the bus. I didn't have to get on the bus and deal with the stares, looks and just the feeling of being alone. It seemed to be off to a good start. When I walked through the door of the school and into the hallway suddenly, I started to feel sick. My head started spinning. It seemed like the walls were closing in on me. Anxiety came over me like this rushing wind. I started walking down the hallway. The noise from the kids seemed so loud. The hallway was so busy kids walking, pushing and talking trying to get to class. I was so overwhelmed; I could barely breathe. I thought to myself, I just needed to get to the washroom. When I walked into washroom there was a group of girls standing by the faucet. I began to wash my face and suddenly, I turn and all three were standing there staring. At first, I just put my head down, but then I looked and ask if there was a problem. One of the girls turned to the others and said, "What the Hell happened to her". I'm guessing she thought I didn't hear her, but I did. After I wipe my face, I turned to her and looked directly in her face. Gave her this look, asked her if she needed me to answer some questions. I told her you seemed curious about something. I mean you asked "What the HELL happened to me" so I thought I would help you. The look on her face was priceless. I then turned and walk out. As I slowly walked down the hallway to class, keeping my head down, I didn't want to make eye contact with anyone who would say something or cause me to say something. I didn't want to see the looks on the other kids' faces as they watched me like I was a walking disease. As I'm walking to my first class. I finally saw someone that looked familiar. We went to class together. After going to a few of my classes and walking around the school, I started seeing more of my friends from elementary school. I was becoming more comfortable and less

THE DARK SIDE THAT BIRTHED MY WORSHIP

fearful. The remainder of the day for the most part was ok. I made it through my first day. Now it's time for me to go home and I had to catch the bus. Initially when I left the school, I was looking for the guys that I rode to school with. Hoping to see them so I didn't have to get on the bus. Once I didn't see them, I began to walk towards the bus stop. Here comes that feeling in the pit of my stomach again. As I was walking toward the bus stop, this guy walks past me and says, "What's wrong with your face?" I looked at him and said, "What's wrong with your face?" He looked at me and start to laugh. My friend grabbed me and told me to get on the bus. I got on the bus, and she hugged me. "Don't worry about him, he's stupid,". I acted as if I didn't know what she was talking about and diverted the conversation to something else. As time went on, I developed friendships with some amazing people that supported me in my journey. Not everyone was so nice though. Some of the girls I ran into where very nasty to me and treated me like I was disgusting. I had to develop this tough skin to let them know I wasn't the one to play with. There were days I would come home full of rage because of how some of the girls treated me. Other times I would come home so broken from experiencing the ignorance of people on the bus and their reaction towards me. One day at school, I was walking through the hallway, I walked past this guy that gave me the scariest look ever. It would be right after my fifth period class. He would walk past me in the halls and say, "You Ugly as Hell". He was so scary looking. One of the worst kids in school. He was so angry and just mean to me for no reason. I didn't see him every day but when I did it would be in passing. He would say the most hurtful things. One day I was walking to class and he was coming towards me. The closer he got the more scared I was, because I never knew what he was going to say. For some reason I wouldn't open my mouth to defend myself when it came to this guy. I wasn't afraid of the girls but this guy I was afraid of. One day he walked past me with a group of guys and yelled out "here comes SPOTS". They all laughed and started calling me spots. I just kept walking with my head down. I felt horrible inside. I wanted to disappear. I had that same feeling I did the night of the dance. For some reason when it came to this guy I would freeze up. This guy used to taunt and bully me for a long time. I was called "spots" most of the time. He also called me "burn face" and "skinny ugly." I buried the tears trying not to let it bother me. It got so bad I would walk the other way to get to class so I didn't have to run into him. One time I remember after encountering this guy, I left the school and got on the bus. I let the words and cruel stares bother me so much I was ready to break down. I tried to avoid this person as much as I could until I couldn't anymore. I remember one day during my sophomore year, the hall bell ranged. I came out of the room and was walking to my next class. And there he was! I could see him from afar coming towards me. My stomach began to form butterflies with fear. My head slowly started to sink down. The closer he got, the more I felt myself sinking. But then, something came over me, and I had this feeling of "no more." When he got nearer, he opened his mouth and yelled, "Look, here come spots!" I stopped in my tracks and looked at him and shouted, "Oh my God, your breath stinks! Ugh, you dirty." While saying this, I'm pointing at him, so now the attention is on him. Remember the hallways are crowded with students, so they all looked and began laughing so hard. He tried to come for me but another dude grabs him and said not her. I was so fed up I was ready for whatever with him. That day was a win for me. He just stood there looking crazy. Maybe he was in shock I don't know. A level of confidence came over me. I was tired. I wasn't going to take it anymore from this dude. He had me afraid for over a year and I just couldn't take it anymore. After that happened, I went on to my next class. After that when I saw him again, he would just walk pass me, but he would not say a word. This too I kept to myself because I was scared and didn't know what to do. I never spoke about this guy, that bullied and taunt me in school to anyone. I would go on to school every day and was ridiculed by this boy but came home and acted as if my day went so well. Even my good friends that I was in school with didn't know of the guy and how he would bother me every day. I never encountered a bully again in school.

CHAPTER 8
THE BIRTHING
THE ENCOUNTER

Overall, my high school years were as normal as possible besides the bully that tormented me for a while. I remember one night; I was mentally drained. I got ready for bed as usual after my bath. As I lay there to go to sleep, I began to hear voices in my head. Those moments in school began to play in my head. The voices began to sound just like him. The guy that taunted and bullied me in school. "I told you, you were ugly, you just a spotted girl. You need to cover your face because nobody wants to be around you." I could hear him whispering in my ear calling me burn face, spots, racoon face. The more I tried to cover my ears and go to sleep, the louder I could hear his voice. I sat up at the top of my headboard and just sat there. Those thoughts can torment you even after you no longer encounter the person. I remember getting up and getting on my knees. I turned my little radio on and began to listen to Yolanda Adams "The Battle is Not Yours." I would lay across my bed and listen to this song often when other things were going on in the house as well. This was my way to escape. It was embedded in my heart. As I was on my knees, I began to feel the aching in my heart.

I began to pray. I always started with Psalms 23; this is the first prayer I learned from youth Bible school. The youth church played a big part in my spiritual growth and most of the learning I received, I still carry in my heart today. So, I developed a prayer life at a very young age. Praying palms 23, Psalms 91 and the lord's model prayer became a routine for me. Something different happened this night. Later I realized praying in this manner I was building an altar of prayer. The little girl within constantly cried out by screaming, scratching herself, closing herself off to the world inwardly, trying to convince me that my life wasn't worth living with this ugly disease. The only way to silence her was to pray. Those three prayers were all I knew at the time and all I would pray. If I wasn't praying, I was asking God a million times to take this feeling away. When I wasn't asking God to take this feeling away, I was listening to the voice in my mind trying to keep me in this low sinking place. I often felt so helpless trying to understand it all but this night something was different. I was crying out to him. I was in this place of feeling so low and unwanted, I needed God to hear my pain and anguish. I just wanted this feeling to leave completely. While praying the song by Yolanda Adams was playing in background, suddenly, a sound came out of my belly that scared me to pieces. I

THE DARK SIDE THAT BIRTHED MY WORSHIP

jumped up and looked around the room. It was dark, and I was shaking so hysterically. I started praying again, and there it goes again. This sound I never heard before, and it's coming from my mouth. The best way I could describe it, like when a baby tries to talk, and "blabber" comes out. This scared me so much that I didn't know how to finish praying. I sat there on my knees in complete silence trying to make sense of what just happened. It was an unknown sound that didn't make sense. I was afraid to pray after that. I tried to pray some more and there it goes again this sound. I was so afraid I just got up and got in my bed. From that night on, my life had changed. That night I was filled with the Holy Spirit with the evidence of speaking in tongues. I had a little knowledge even as a young as I was but didn't come into the full knowledge of it until I was a little older. I thought to myself, I couldn't tell anyone. I didn't want people laughing at me or thinking I'm crazy. I didn't know how to articulate what was going on with me. I didn't say anything to anyone because I was too afraid. I was already different and to add this to my plate would have taken me over to say the least. Not to mention that a burning feeling went through my body at the same time this sound came from my mouth. The feeling is hard to describe. The best way I can describe it is when something extremely hot touches your finger, and you feel it through your entire body. That's how I felt. As I laid in my bed, I was thinking to myself what just happened. I remember there was a prophet at my church that I heard speak in this language but never really got a true understanding of what a prophet was either, so I was afraid to approach her. After that night my curiosity started hounding me. I found myself trying to make sense of what happened that night. I also found myself wanting to know more about the prophet in our church. I was afraid of her, but at the same time, I wanted to get close to her. Back then, I was just a young teenager that didn't know a lot about the Holy Spirit, and it wasn't being taught in my church. Although I was afraid of the prophet, for some reason, I was drawn to her. I would watch her as she would pray and speak in the unknown language. I watched how she served God without any care to what the people thought about her. She didn't care who was looking or staring at her. She did some things that seemed strange or unusual. Since that night, I was searching for answers. One thing for sure, her and a couple of the other mothers spoke this language I spoke that night. After a while I began to gravitate towards them and began to seek out the things of God concerning the Holy Spirit. I was only a teenager, and the only girl that spoke it

THE DARK SIDE THAT BIRTHED MY WORSHIP

to my knowledge, so I couldn't tell anyone. I was already "the strange girl," "the girl that stood out," I didn't want to be called the "weird girl" either. This hunger to understand and know what this was and find out what was happening to me got stronger. One day I spoke to the Rev, trying to figure out what was happening to me. I never said anything to my parents, I was too afraid. I didn't think they would understand because they weren't in church like that. I would hear certain statements about people who spoke in tongues not being real. There were times I would be around others that made a mockery out it and those who spoke it. The only person I knew to talk about this with was Rev. I had always kept this part of my life from them, afraid of what they would do or say. That night changed my life. I believe this was the awakening of the worshipper within. I began to see things differently. I began to hear things differently. Everything changed after that night. I never was the same. I found myself praying and in the mist of me prayer this language would come forth. I would close my mouth thinking it would go away, but it never did. It became more stronger the more I prayed. One thing I noticed as time went on, instead of crying out to God about my pain or allowing the little girl to create this battle in my mind. I would replace that with this unknown language. My questions to God went from why is this happening to me to what is happening to me?

CHAPTER 9
THE TURNING POINT

I felt like my life was going through another turn. I'm still dealing with the ugliness of the world. The patches began to spread even more, now more stares and looks. People started asking me if I had been in a fire. At this point I was mentally, and emotionally drained. Although I had a great group of friends around me that treated and supported me despite my condition. I still dealt with the bullying and constantly defending myself from the kids that felt they could openly say what they felt. Many days I'd ride the bus and sit in the front, in the back of the bus the other kids from school sat in the back. They would make jokes or sit in the corner and literally have a complete conversation about me. Some would make fun of me right in my face. This was becoming so overwhelming. This became my norm. One moment I'm enjoying the festivities of school and the next I'm holding back tears. So, church for me played a very important part my life. Without it I'm sure I would have lost my mind. My faith was in God totally. With everything I was learning in church, I had to believe he was going to change my skin back and I could live a normal life. I had to believe that God was going to heal me and that the brokenness I felt was going to go away. Not just the problem with my skin but that I would receive the love and support of a mother that I so desired. I had to believe that one day I was going to make her proud of me as her daughter, and not feel like I was a mistake. These things I had my hope in, so church was very important. Not only that church was the place I could get the answers I was looking for, but the place I could release all my emotion through song. In my mind I felt I was in a whirlwind. One day in rehearsal at the church my God mother gave me a song to learn. She told me she wanted me to sing it. I was completely nervous and scared. I went home and began to listen to the song. It was titled "Speak to My Heart" by Donnie McClurkin. I would listen to it so much I would fall asleep with my headphones on with the song playing in my ears. That next Saturday was the day we would rehearse the song. I was completely nervous, and fear was all over me. Remember, after that night I prayed in an unknown language I was never the same. Now I'm here in rehearsal and we are going over this song with the choir. When it came time for me to sing the lead part, I opened my mouth, nothing came out. She stops then tells me to try again. I open my mouth and I could feel the trembling in my voice. She looked at me and told me to close my eyes and just sing to God. The moment I closed my eyes and

THE DARK SIDE THAT BIRTHED MY WORSHIP

open my mouth, I got lost in the song. It was no longer about who was watching me. I was lost in the presence of God. I felt as if it was just me and him. I felt something lift from my shoulder in this moment, even as a teenager, I could feel the tears falling from my eyes and I could feel this peace come over me in this moment. All I remember was opening my eyes and the director came to me, and she hugged me so hard. She said, "Thank you." And she kept hugging me. Tears were flowing down my eyes as it was with everyone else in the choir. This was my first worship experience as a little girl through song. I can't explain the feeling that went through my body. In that moment, it was just Him and me. In that moment, I saw a little girl. A little girl that was pain-free and made whole inside and out. All I saw was a light shining and a little girl going up. In that moment it was like I knew everything was ok. This was an encounter with God and the effects of being in His presence. I didn't want this feeling to go away. In the moment I didn't feel weighted down, nor did I worry. I felt peace, joy, and the warmth of his presence. The feeling in the back of my throat was gone. My tears didn't hurt but healed in that moment. Of course, then I didn't understand what that meant, but now I do. For me, this was the place where the focus was not an emotional detachment that I often revert back to. While I was going through this change in my life as an early teen, I found myself drawn to prayer and meditation. I gravitated towards the mothers of the church that prayed openly. I would sit with them and watch during alter prayer. I would observe everything about them when it came to pray and moving in the holy spirit. I believe this was the beginning of being able to identify the birthing of the worshipper that lied within. I still was battling the stress of my pigment changing right before me. The difference this time is I began to learn how to channel that energy of anger, hurt, rejection and low self-esteem, put it into a song of worship.

(The secret place)

Psalms 91 a powerful passage or scripture to meditate on when you are in a place that you feel you can't come back from. The first verse alone describes the place where God found me. The word that captured me the most is the "secret place." We often think secrets are a bad thing. When you have a secret, you are hiding something, and most times you believe it's something bad or so embarrassing or shameful you don't want anyone to know of it. When you look up the definition of the word "secret" in the Hebrew language. It states it is to a secret intimate friendship.

THE DARK SIDE THAT BIRTHED MY WORSHIP

Wow, that phrase alone speaks volumes. Some of the acronyms for "secret" found in the Thesaurus are classified: covered, mysterious, unseen, cryptic, deep, and dark. These are just a few of the many. I hope you are getting the picture. This word is so loaded. For me, I found the meaning of this word through the "dark." I took all the hurt, shame, embarrassment, self-hatred, self-rejection, and the blame I felt towards God, myself, parents and those around and release it in this dark place. It was FEAR that tried to rob me of life. In this place, I thought I was just expressing it all. What God revealed to me is that I was giving it all to Him in the secret place. When the scriptures say, "Cast all your cares upon me," that is exactly what I was doing, and I didn't realize it. One thing I failed to mention, many nights me crying out was not just about my pigment but also the verbal abuse received from my mother. Weekends were the worst. I will never forget this particular night. I came home from rehearsal, and I went to my room to put my things up. I went into the kitchen to grab something to eat. I walked past the family area, and my parents were there listening to music and having adult time. As I walked up the hallway to my room, immediately, my mom started attacking me. I went to my brothers' room, sat on the bed, laughing and talking to them and then she came in and began saying things about me that were so hurtful and untrue. She talked about me always being around my brothers and their friends and instructed me to go into my room. She would scream for no reason. She told me I didn't have any business being in their room. As I was walking back to my room, she pushed me up against the wall and was just saying things a mother should not say to a daughter. I was around fifteen years old at the time. I remember looking up and calling on the name of Jesus. Pinned to the corner of the hallway. She got in my face, screaming again. My dad came up the hall and told her to get off me and asked her what she was doing. I proceeded to walk away, and she grabs me. I fell to my knees and just called on the name of Jesus. I just wanted the yelling to stop. The more I called on His name, the more she got loud and then mocked me by saying, "Call on Jesus, and I will wait until He comes." Then she began to ask me whether she knew God or not. I wasn't sure what she meant by that. She told me that without her, I wouldn't know anything about Jesus. It's because of her that I knew Him. I hated my life. I felt punished or something. I never understood why I was always attacked. I asked myself what I do so bad for her to always come down on me for no reason. All I could think about in that moment was if I could just get to the door

THE DARK SIDE THAT BIRTHED MY WORSHIP

and go to my granny's, I would be okay. Other than facing the world and the anger people often express towards me, I was battling the demons in my home as well.

(The 1st Prophesy)

Again, I am taking you on a journey with me in hopes of showing you how God took what the enemy used for bad and turned it around for my good. The encounters that I faced growing with this disease only pushed and prepared me for my destiny and purpose that God has for me. I was just a teenager, and all I knew was there was a language that didn't make sense to me, and it would come forth in the night during my moments of tears and sorrow, anguish and pain.

I will never forget the moment as if it was yesterday. I will never forget the words that came from what I now know as one of the prophets of God. One Sunday, during youth class, one of the ushers came to get me. He said, "they want you upstairs". At first, I'm looking at him as if he wasn't talking to me directly. I then asked, "Who wants to see me upstairs and for what?" He told me again, "They want you upstairs." I got up to go upstairs through the back, and the usher then said, "No, go through the front. The pastor office goes through that way." In my mind, I'm thinking, "What the heck is going on? So, I did as I was instructed. When I got up the stairs, there was a lady that was prophesying over the church. I had never seen her or met her. So, I got upstairs, and I am standing off to the side against the wall. My hands were shaking out of control. I still didn't know who called me and why I was needed. I didn't know anything. The next thing I know, that same lady that was prophesying over the church turned and instructed me to come to her. I stood there for a hot second. My body was stuck, and I couldn't move. She stood before me and said, "God wants to speak to you." She began to prophesy and said, "God has favored you." Here I am, at fifteen standing in front of the entire church, and she says this over the microphone. My first instinct was to run away and hide, not just from her but from the church because I'm sure my face was completely red, and I was completely embarrassed. I didn't know much about prophets, prophesy or anything of that nature. There was no one in the church that could make sense of it, the few that did know didn't say anything. She scared me. I was shaking in my legs. So, I closed my eyes, and I began to listen to the words she was speaking over me. She continued to say, "God has favored you." She continued. "God will make your name great, and when you speak, it will cause breakthroughs in people's life." A part

THE DARK SIDE THAT BIRTHED MY WORSHIP

of me was so confused, the other part of me was an emotional wreck. Once she was done speaking what the Lord said, I lifted my hands, and I just cried. The weight of His glory was so heavy on me that the only thing I could do was fall to my knees and cry. I didn't know what to do or say. I was speechless and confused at the same time. So, when I came home, it was something I couldn't talk about because I didn't know how to. Imagine standing in front of an entire church as a young girl and called out of the congregation and a stranger comes before you and begins to speak things about you, that would cause you to almost look crazy. Imagine this moment happening to you at a young age, but your parents are nowhere to be found. God always does things for a reason. There were two people who were always there during the times God would call me out and speak my grandmother and my auntie. Although my grandmother didn't understand what was going on when it came to speaking in a heavenly language and prophesying, she did listen to my heart. She did hold me after and wiped my tears. I am grateful because of the comfort she provided me after I knew something was changing within me and I was feeling different. She was there to hold me. After church, when I got home, I went to my room. I laid across my bed and just allowed the word of the prophet to play over and over in my head. I wasn't home alone; I just had no one to talk to about it. My mom was so busy playing her blues and hanging with her girlfriends and my dad at this time was leaving for work. I buried this public encounter inside, and no one in my household ever knew about this wonderful but confusing experience. I honestly thought no one would understand, and I was terrified to say anything about it. This experience changed my entire life. I believe this moment and that prophesy on one hand, opened my eyes even the more on the other hand, I became so fearful. I was afraid of what people would think of me if I openly said what I heard God say to me. I started having dreams even more, what I now know to be visions that would fully manifest. I was terrified of what my parents would think of me. I will never forget the time I came home from church during the weekend. My mother was intoxicated, and she began to scold me for something I didn't do or had any knowledge of. She was screaming in my face. I inwardly called on the name of Jesus, all of a sudden, she stops yelling. It was like nothing had just happened. She went back to what she was doing with her friends. I got up, and I went into my room. I turned on my radio to my favorite song. Then suddenly, my mother came into the room, and snatches the radio from me and

THE DARK SIDE THAT BIRTHED MY WORSHIP

told me I don't need a radio and Yolanda doesn't know what she is talking about. She slammed my room door behind her as she left my room. I laid there in total darkness. I couldn't understand why this was happening to me. I was looking up in the dark asking God why He didn't save me from this woman. I started telling myself that she hated and despised me for being her daughter. I asked God, "What did I ever do to deserve this?" I kept asking myself what it was about me that made her so angry at me. Why did she treat me like I wasn't a part of her? I was a straight A honor roll student, I did my chores, and all I did was go to church. If I wasn't at church, I was next door with my cousins or somewhere on the block. But until later in my teenage years, I was one who stayed at home and was a pretty good kid, so I thought. I could not understand what was it about me that made her treat me the way she did. Then this little small voice began to speak to me. As I was looking in the ceiling, I asked myself did she really feel this way? I ask myself. I didn't want to believe this to be true. He didn't save me from her and that I was stuck with her. I told Him that she was evil and how could He make her my mother. I was so confused about how I could love God so hard, and He allows these things to happen to me. Not only do I have to fight people that I encounter every day, but I also have to fight my own mother and the hatred she had for me. This was so hard for me to understand. I needed to be wanted by her. I needed the love of a mother. I needed to be heard. I never was. The older I got the more difficult it became living at home. Now again, I loved church, and I would go to church either with the youth pastor, my grandmother or godmother. Sometimes, my brother and I would walk. But nothing I did felt like it was enough that would fill that void. While lying there in total darkness. No music playing in the background. Just me and my mind. Praying silently, suddenly, a light began to shine over my face. I open my eyes and nothing. Closed my eyes again and there goes this light. While praying, hears comes this language. Remember this language I didn't ask for, but God chose to give it to me. This heavenly language was flowing. This night I couldn't stop. When I opened my mouth, the words were coming forth. I couldn't stop myself, even when I tried to cover my mouth with my hands. Tears began to come from my eyes, and I found myself crying so much until I couldn't breathe. I was being transformed into who God wanted me to be right in those moments. I began to cry out to God even more because not only did I feel like I was fighting while awake, I was fighting while asleep. The dreams I was having were becoming

THE DARK SIDE THAT BIRTHED MY WORSHIP

violent. There were nights I would avoid going to sleep so that I wouldn't have the dreams. I didn't understand, and I wanted all this to stop. My mind in the dark now became a war zone. I was fighting myself against the enemy. When that prophecy went forth and released in the earth, Satan, right at that moment sent his demons to try to destroy that very word. He knew this door was the beginning of me being open and I was getting ready to seek out the things of God. The dreams I was having were of me being chased. In this dream, I would be running so fast down this dark and long road, and he would be so close that I would almost get caught. Then I wake up jumping and shaking so bad. One day, I got tired of having this dream and not knowing what it meant. I went to church and talked to Rev. I talked to him and told him about the dream. I told him when it started and asked why or what it meant. He then sat me down and began to ask me questions pertaining to the dream and what was going on at home. I gave him all the details. And then he told me that the enemy was trying to stop me from being set free. He's trying to stop God's plan for my life. Rev told me not to worry and gave me certain scriptures to pray and make declarations over my mind right before I go to bed. The Bible tells us in John 10:10, that the enemy comes to steal, kill and destroy and his job is to do that by any means necessary. Once the enemy has a glimpse of your future, it's his job to try to destroy you before you reach your destiny, or you become awaked. The enemy knows that if he stops, delays or denies you of reaching, pursuing or walking in your purpose, others will not come into their purpose either. This is why I almost came to the point of death when I tried to end my life. He tried to take me with low self-esteem, rejection, isolation and put me to shame with embarrassment. He tried to take my mind with depression, fear and the illusion that I was okay when I was not. I'm not this person," I thought to myself. I'm not this church girl. I wanted to be like the other girls and hang out do things that church girls don't do. So, I began to pursue that. Still looking to fill this void. This time it was in all the wrong places.

CHAPTER 10
REJECTION

I was sixteen years old and I was a junior in high school when I got my first real job. I worked at McDonald's in the North Western train station. I was so excited to start working. I can remember my first day at work. The people were so friendly and very nice. I remember meeting so many different people. I had a couple of classmates that worked at the same place. So, I felt a little comfortable working there. I started out working in the back area. In the back area, you didn't really have to interact with customers. I worked on the line and didn't have to come to the front of the store. So, I was safe. I didn't have to worry about the stares and looks from the people. I didn't have to worry about explaining myself. Well one day, that all changed. I came to work, and my manager told me that she was going to have someone train me on the cash register. Initially, I was excited because I was learning something new. Then fear and anxiety began to kick in. This overwhelming feeling made me afraid to do it. One thing about me, I'm good as long as I'm in the background and I'm not forced to talk to people or get put in front street. The moment you put me in front or have me speak before someone, fear and anxiety would overtake me. As I said at the beginning of this chapter, I worked downtown at the North Western train station. This is one of the busiest train stations in downtown Chicago and is used by people from all walks of life. I was training on the cash register, and I took a customer order. I could see from a distance that the line was building up and there was another customer standing there the entire time just looking at me as I took orders. Now it was time to take her order. For a long time, she stood there stared in my face. "Hello, can I take your order?" I said to greet the customer. She was dead silent, and I didn't get any response. This person stood there for about two minutes looking in my face. Again, I said, "Hello can I take your order?" Then finally the person asked me what happened to my face. Immediately, I could feel anger rising from within. She stood there looking at me waiting for me to answer her question. I wanted to blow up on her, but I realized it was my job. I politely ignored her and asked what she would like to order. She asked me again what had happened to me. I responded and told her nothing. She gave me this look as if I said something offensive to her. So, I gave her the same look. She decided she didn't want me to take her order, so she stepped over to the next line. The manager saw that she moved to another line and therefore came

THE DARK SIDE THAT BIRTHED MY WORSHIP

to ask the lady if something was wrong and why she moved to the next line. She stated she didn't want me to take her order. My manager then goes on to ask if I said or did something wrong that would cause her to feel this way. She told the manager no, but something was wrong with my skin and she didn't want to touch me. I was steaming in rage. At the same time, I was embarrassed. She looked at me as if I was some type of contagious infection. I didn't do anything but my job. This world is filled with people with no compassion for others. Once the line was down and I was able to go to the washroom, I went and closed the door. And I stood there in the mirror, the tears started to come down, but these were tears of anger and rage that I was holding back. I stood there for a while staring at myself. I could see the steam from my nostrils I was so mad. I was turning red in my face. I was so angry, I could scream. I just stood there breathing hard with my eyes closed trying to calm myself down. While my eyes were closed, I could hear this small voice tell me that I am greater, I am better than this. I heard the voice tell me to pick my face up and open my eyes, look in the mirror again. At first, I was still with my head down saying this is not worth it. These people are not worth it, this job is not worth it. I began to tell myself if this is what I had to deal with, I'm done. The voice tells me to hold my head up. This time it was so loud, it startled me. I thought it was someone in the washroom with me. I looked up in the mirror. While looking at the mirror, behind me was a light of some sort. This light did not come from the light in the ceiling, but it was behind me. It was behind my right ear. It was so subtle, but I could see it. Then the voice says again that I am greater and better than this. This feeling came over me, and I began to feel at ease. This overwhelming confidence came over me. I wiped my face and pulled myself together and went back to work. This scripture came to my mind: "Greater is He that is in me than He that is in the world." I began to repeat this scripture in my head. The more I said it over in my head, the more I started to feel better about myself and this job. I knew that the light I saw behind my right ear was God and He was reminding me that He was with me. As I continued to say it, my heart was being lifted. As I continued, my character was being built. The more I said it, the more I was silencing the enemy. I was realigning my heart and my thoughts to the God that was in me. I went back to the front of the store. I had a beautiful smile on my face, and as the next customer was approaching, I had a different attitude. What happened was that the spirit within came over me, and I began to operate in the spirit.

THE DARK SIDE THAT BIRTHED MY WORSHIP

I didn't look at the person, I looked at how I can serve that person without stepping out of character because they didn't understand me. I operated from a different place. This was my posture when I went to work. Not only to work but everywhere I went. I began to see through people when they approached me or stare at my face. Not every day was a good day, but I was learning how to control my inner emotions when I did have those not so good days. The bad days consisted of people not wanting to get in my line of service or when someone would not want to touch my hand and therefore put their money on the countertop and look at me to pick it up. Now don't get me wrong, I had those moments where I would have to be pulled to the side and spoken to by my supervisor. There were times I would go back and forth with a customer, but for the most part, I stood my ground. Those who had children would stare and ask questions and they would be rude enough to try to answer their kids with ignorant responses, but I just tried my best to control my attitude and see past the racism and discrimination. God allowed me to see some things on this job. For instance, He allowed me to see how cruel even adults can be. But at this point, I knew enough about God that helped me to shut myself off and still be working at the same time. This job built my character and helped me know what I would have to face in this world as I encountered many people from many walks of life. One day at work, there was a guy that I noticed would only come and sit out in the lobby. This guy would sit there until the close of the restaurant. At first, I didn't realize it was as often as it was. One day, one of my colleagues pulled me to the side to tell me know that guy was asking about me. I was confused and didn't understand why because I had never seen this person before in my life. I acted as if I didn't hear what she said and continued to do my job. This guy waited until the place was closing and finally decided he was going to approach me. He walked up to my line as if he was going to order something. Once he was at my register, he asked for my name. Luckily, we didn't wear name tags. I decided to give him a fake name. As the days went by, he started showing up all the time, even on my off days. I never said anything else to this person other than stating to him my fake name. One night, we began to have conversations. He would often just stare at my face and eyes. Of course, at first, I'm giving him the look like I'm ready to go off and then he would give me compliments. He would tell me how beautiful I was and how he loves to look at my face. One day, when I was leaving work, he followed me and realized that I took public

THE DARK SIDE THAT BIRTHED MY WORSHIP

transportation. I didn't know he was following me, but I later found out that he followed the bus to where I would get off the bus. Now I want you to picture this. I am only around sixteen years old and I would get off work sometimes after 11 pm. I would have to take the train and bus home by myself. Some days, my brother would meet me at the bus stop, and other days, my friends from the neighborhood would meet me. But most nights, I would walk home by myself. One night, he came to the store waiting around as usual. Now for me, this was becoming a nice thing. Someone noticed me and told me all the things a girl would want to hear. He made me feel special just by showing me attention. Even with all that, I saw darkness when I looked in his face. It was something behind his eyes. I didn't understand it or I was just blind to see it. The eyes would always cause me to hesitate when he would ask me a personal question. One night, as I closed the store and was about leaving, he was still there waiting. After walking out, he asked me if he could take me home. At first, I declined. He insisted on making sure I got home. I finally gave in and got in the car. Wait! I failed to mention this person was very much older than me. While riding home, we talked, and I asked about what he does for a living. He told me he had just gotten back in town not too long ago and he was trying to get his life back in order. Immediately, I felt like someone punched me in the stomach. At this point, I got quiet and was looking out the window trying to figure out how can I get out this car. After a few minutes of dead silence, he asked if I was okay. I told him I was, and I just wanted to get home because I had class the next day and that I was tired. He said, "I need you to run somewhere with me." Immediately, I was terrified. I told him I had to get home, and my parents were waiting for me. He gave me this look, and all I remember was the darkness I saw in his eyes. Next thing I know, we are way past my friend's house which is where I told him to take me. I wanted him to think he was taking me home, but he was taking me to someone else's house because I didn't want him to know where I lived. He pulls over and then turns the car off. I sat looking out the window, and I began to start praying. He asked me if I wanted to know where he was out of town. I told him no, I just needed to get home. I think he could sense the fear in me. At this point, the look on my face was blank. I started praying under my breathe. I prayed that God would let this man let me go so I can go home. All of a sudden, he reaches over to try to kiss me. I refused and just said I had to go home. He got so angry and hit the dashboard. This rage and anger came out of nowhere. I started

THE DARK SIDE THAT BIRTHED MY WORSHIP

praying harder and harder. I screamed, and he grabbed me and said, "No one is going to love you like I do." I said in fear, "I don't even know you and how do you love me? I just met you." At this point, I knew my life was in complete danger. He then turns to me, and says, "No one is going to want you because you are ugly, no one is going to want to take you in public." He started saying all these cruel things to me. I jumped out of the car and started running down the street. He got out and started chasing me. He decided to get back in his car and started chasing me with it. I was running as fast as I could. Luckily, I was close to my house. The guys on the block were outside I ran straight to them. I told them that someone was chasing me, and they immediately hid me in one of the buildings they ran. When this guy pulls up and tries to jump out the car, one of the guys out there told him it would be in his best interest to leave and never come back. My heart was pounding in my chest. I was terrified. I stayed in the building for a long time and then one of the guys took me home. When I got in the house, I went straight to my room shaking. I locked the door, and I began to cry and scream uncontrollably. I couldn't believe what happened. How on earth did I let this happen? I started blaming myself for being so vulnerable. As I laid in my bed, that little girl's voice began to talk loudly, "You are stupid and dumb. How can you ever think that someone would really like you? Did you really think that you could be seen in public with someone? No. Face it, you are pitiful. All I could think about is what could have happened. I could have been raped or killed. I was so afraid and couldn't believe this happened. She kept talking, so I got up and just sat up in my bed. I sat up in the dark and began to thank God over and over again. I couldn't stop thanking Him for keeping me and letting me get home. I could only imagine what could have happened to me, so I began to thank Him even more. As I was thanking Him and sitting in my bed, I began to hear this still voice tell me, "I was always there. I was always there and will always be there." I then asked, "Well, what about the cruel things that were said to me. I didn't do anything to deserve this God." He began to tell me about the caterpillar and the butterfly. This was going on right in my room. When I show you to the world, you are going to be simply beautiful in all men eyes. He reminded me of what he spoke to me through the woman of God when I was fourteen years old. Then he began to tell me how I would be one to change the way people love and see me. He also began to tell me that generational curses would be broken, and my family would be healed. I laid down and allowed God's sweet spirit

THE DARK SIDE THAT BIRTHED MY WORSHIP

to minister to me. It felt like His arms were wrapped around me, as I laid there. He was wiping all my tears and pain away. I fell asleep like a baby in the arms of her mother. I never told anyone about what happened to me that night, and I never saw this person again.

CHAPTER 11
I ALMOST LET GO

While pursuing the things of God, going to church being involved in the youth ministry and just growing in God. I still found myself having this need to be accepted. I wanted to be the girl that fit in so bad. I found myself getting involved with the things of this world. I didn't want to be the spotted girl that all she does is go to church. I was different enough I didn't want to be labeled "The Church Girl". Seeking to be so normal I began to involve myself in the things of this world. I gave my purity away to someone that was not trying to take it. What I mean by that is, I was the one that pressured him into having sex and not the other way around. I thought if I could lose my virginity like my friends, I would be cool and people wouldn't think I wasn't wanted. I was trying to fill this void of emptiness that I thought I could only get by giving up my body. I thought if I do this and show that I am down, then we wouldn't have to talk about why I look the way I did. "It's okay for him to call me raccoon face because he was giving me money". This person felt like as long as he was buying me shoes and clothes that, he could treat me any type of way. Another dark side I lived in. No one knows the evil streak that this person had, except me I thought it

THE DARK SIDE THAT BIRTHED MY WORSHIP

was love. I was belittled so many times. Made to feel like this was the way I was supposed to be treated. What happens to many of us, we bury ourselves in the things of this world, looking for love in all the wrong places. This was another fight I was battling in my mind. Asking myself is this what love supposed to feel like? This was killing me on the inside: living a life of perversion to cover up the complete disappointment of my outer appearance, wearing a mask that was deteriorating from the inside out. It was like I was living a double almost triple life. Again, this is what happens to so many young girls, we feel like we need to fill this void that ultimately only God can fill. We give ourselves away, and we lose ourselves in the lust of our flesh even being a church girl. We know the truth, but we try so hard not to be that person while trying to fit in. I was going in so deep, and no one would have known I learned how to wear a mask. I learned how to smile when I wanted to cry. I learned how to laugh when I wanted to scream. I learned how to cover up the scars from cutting myself. Many nights I would come home from work after being treated like I was a disease by the customers I encounter. Even then, I learned how to wear the mask. A lot of us live this delusion as if everything is ok, but in reality, we put this mask on to cover up. I found myself moving away from the things of God more and more. I got away from praying and spending time with my Father. It seems like that hunger and thirst I had for the things of God was slowly going way. I got to a place where I wouldn't cry out to him anymore. I still would get upset when I would go certain places, but I hid those emotions. I got to the place where I shielded away from the mirror so I wouldn't have to see myself. The reality is I wasn't normal. I call myself in love but, he was wearing a mask just as I was. No matter what I did, it never seemed to work. I would end up more broken, rejected and alone, but to cover that up I lost myself more and more. I became this person that would hurt you before you hurt me. I was losing the uniqueness of myself. I was losing the hope that God was going to fix me. I was giving up on the idea that I could be healed and that my skin pigment could go back to the way it was when I was born. While giving up the hope of it, I was becoming angrier inside. I was confused. My mind was in a state of emotional dysfunction. I buried all this in, by trying to live a life that was not mine. One day, I met a guy. He was older than me. He seemed very nice and kind. Told me all the things I wanted to hear. But he was the devil in disguise. I met up with him by my house, and we hung out together. We were about to go to the corner store when I decided I wanted to go

THE DARK SIDE THAT BIRTHED MY WORSHIP

to a different store. He insisted on going that way to the other store, but I insisted on going in the opposite direction. Eventually the guy caught on to what I was doing. He figured out that I was trying to avoid something. Then it happened. As we were walking, he started asking me questions. Weird questions. I started getting nervous. Then he started talking about violent things. He started telling me about his past and the cruel things he did in the past. By this time, I was terrified. I started to turn around and go back home. I told him I needed to get something I left. He decides to grab me around my neck. I couldn't scream; I couldn't do anything. He tells me that I shouldn't play games with people. I decided to knee him, and I started running. But he caught up to me as I ran trying to get to my friend's house. He grabbed me and picked me up, threw me to the ground and got on top of me to hold me down. This was happening in the middle of the day, in the back of my house, in an alley. While holding me down, he tells me how he only wanted to see what a black/ white (____) well, you know, feels like. He told me he thought I was the ugliest thing walking around and he was going to throw me out once he got what he wanted. He told me that no one would ever want to be seen in public with me and that I looked like a freak. I tried to scream but couldn't. I was only a couple of feet away from my best friend's back door. The door was open, but I couldn't do anything. He finally lets me up and told me to walk with him. He took me to this abandoned building. I was terrified. I was looking at death's door again. This time it wasn't by my own hand. I thought he was going to kill me and leave me there. He pushed me up against the wall and began to molest me. I stood there so helpless. He took his tongue and licked my face. I tried to fight, but the way I was pinned I couldn't move. Under my breathe I began to say Jesus. I didn't stop saying that name. Then that other language came forth. At first, he couldn't hear me. Then while fondling my body he got closer to my face. He looks at me in my eyes and it was if he saw a ghost. He then got closer to my mouth and began to ask me what I was saying. I didn't stop I just kept calling Jesus and speaking in this divine language. He stepped back to fix his pants and slowly walks away. He didn't take his eyes off my face. He just walked away and didn't look back. I was standing there; I felt my entire heart rip right from my chest. He left me there in this abandoned building. The last words he said before completely vanishing, was that I was disgusting, I wasn't worth it, and something was wrong with me. I just cried. I had enough strength to get up and I ran to my friend's house. When I got to the

THE DARK SIDE THAT BIRTHED MY WORSHIP

back door, I tried to straighten my face up. When I walked in, she asks what was wrong? I just told her I got into an argument with my mother. She kept watching me. She knew it was something else. The way I was shaking, she knew it was something. She asks me again and I just sat there staring into space. She came over and sat next to me. We both just sat there. She didn't say anything, and I didn't either. She looked at me and said, "G we gone make it through this I promise." I put my head on her shoulder and just release all the tears I had left in me. When I got to my home, I opened the door to my room. I lay across my bed; I was so numb I didn't know what to do. I went to the washroom to take a bath. I got in the water, and I soaked myself. I soaked and soaked until I found myself slipping away under the water. You would have thought someone snatched me right out the tub. I began to tell the Lord how sorry I was and how thankful I was that He didn't let me die. I could have died in the abandoned building, but he covered me. The tears would not stop coming, but God didn't let me die, because if I did, I wouldn't be here to tell you "I overcame." God saved me once again. I went to my room, as I laid there, He whisper to me, "Come back, you are not too far gone." He reminded me of His word that says,

Isaiah 59:1 (NIV)
Surely the arm of the Lord is not too short to save,
nor his ear too dull to hear.

CHAPTER 12
THE FINDINGS

Today was the start of a new milestone in my life. I woke up feeling refreshed and ready to conquer this year. My senior year was going to be the best year of my life. I went through the last three years of school with good days but a lot of bad days. I fought a lot of battles in my mind. I tried to bury what happened by never talking about it. I tried to bury those images out of my mind by keeping myself distracted and busy. After that day of horror, I found myself getting back to the place of pursuing the things of God. I started back praying more consistently. I was still wrestling with that little girl within, but I was surviving. I was living. I was surviving high school despite the bullying, rejection and those moments that haunted me. All in all, I made it to my senior year. I was still working downtown for McDonald's and making my own money. This was my last year of high school. My major was Fashion Design. My friends and I had plans to move to another state and become famous designers. I was doing things on my own and for myself. Still involved in church and learning the things of the Holy Spirit. I was still searching for understanding. I was getting back to the place of studying his word more. Things seemed to be going good for me. My confidence level was increasing, and I was comfortable in the skin I was in. The pigment was continuing to progress, but I was in a good place. It was almost as if I was burying my inner emotions. Honestly, everything about my skin I suppressed I didn't focus on covering up anymore. I stop looking for new spots every morning. It was to the point I didn't look in the mirror anymore. I found myself getting tired all the time. My dad told me he made me a doctor's appointment. Without thinking, I said, "Okay." The last time I had been to the doctor was when the doctor told me there was no cure for my skin disorder. The day came for me to go to the doctor. I thought my mother was going to take me, but she didn't. I never understood why it was okay to go to the doctor by myself at seventeen years old, but I guess my mother figured it was. I was pretty independent back then, so I guess it was okay. This was my first appointment to see a Gynecologist, and that would not have been something I wouldn't want my daughter to experience alone. I began to wonder why I needed to go to the doctor. I got off the bus and had no idea where I was going. I walked into the building; I was instructed to go to another building. I got to that building, and again I was sent somewhere else. Finally, I got to the correct building and floor. The

THE DARK SIDE THAT BIRTHED MY WORSHIP

first question I was asked is whether I was alone or not. I was taken to the back to take all kinds of test including a pregnancy test. After a while, the doctor gets the results and tells and me that I am pregnant. I was completely shocked. I sat there in complete disbelief. The doctor then asked me if I lived with my parents. I told her I did she told me I would need to come back for more testing and that I needed to bring a parent with me. My mind was still in shock. I had no idea what she was saying after she mentioned I was nine weeks pregnant. Once the visit was over, I walked to the bus stop to get on the bus to go home. As I was on the bus, all I kept hearing was her voice playing over and over in my head saying I was pregnant. I was completely quiet. As I walked from the bus stop to the house, it felt like I was walking the Green Mile again. My mind was all over the place. I said to God, "I am so sorry." All I kept thinking about was my daddy and how devastated he would be. I felt so alone. No one was there with me. I went to the doctor all alone. I kept on saying to God, I was so sorry. When I came into the house, my mother and brothers were home. I came in and sat down on the floor by the end of the couch. My mother was sleep on the couch. She woke up and asked me how it went at the doctor. I just came right out and told her I was nine weeks pregnant. She jumped up and screamed, "You're pregnant!" My brothers turned to me in astonishment and said, "What?" My mother jumps up and calls my grandmother to see if she had an Ibuprofen, apparently, she got an instant headache. I sat there so quiet; I didn't know what to say or do at that point. My heart was broken because I felt I had let my daddy down. I didn't know how I was going to tell him or face him. As the night went on, all I could hear were my brothers going back and forth about how disappointed they were. They were asking several questions like, "When did this happen? How am I going to finish school now that I'm pregnant?" They just went on and on. I locked myself up in my room and began to cry. As I lay there, here's comes that inner voice, I thought I suppressed. I'm telling myself I cannot have a child. I refuse to have this child. I remember the doctor telling me I needed to decide what I was going to do. I felt so lost, I didn't know what to say or do. I was so disgusted with myself that I cried myself to sleep. My dad came home, and it was as if my body knew. I woke up right when he got home. I could hear my mother talking to him and then my room door opens. I sat up and immediately started crying. He asked me what was wrong and why was crying. I told him because I got pregnant and I had disappointed him. My dad looked at me in the face and told me,

THE DARK SIDE THAT BIRTHED MY WORSHIP

"South Paw, I already knew." I looked at him and said, "Why you didn't tell me?". He laughed so hard. He said, "When I saw your senior pictures, I told your mother then you were pregnant. She didn't believe me, and so I took it upon myself to get you a doctor's appointment." He said, "I knew all along." He then told me we were going to be alright and we don't abort something God allowed to happen. Later that night I had a dream. In that dream, I was in a place with light all around. There was a little girl sitting on the floor. She was holding something in her hands, and she was hugging it so hard. When I came to the front of the little girl, she looked like a baby. The light that was shining so bright in the room covered everything except the little girl. From the back she looked like a little girl, but from the front she had the face of a baby. Then she started to fade away. The room seemed like it was moving away from where I was. The little seemed to get farther away and the light wasn't shining as bright. I woke up from the dream and laid there with my eyes open. While lying there, the enemy started planting thoughts in my mind. All these thoughts about me passing on this disorder that I was living with began to flood my mind. I began to think about what she would have to go through if it was passed on to her. I didn't want her to go through what I was going through. I didn't want her to have to fight like I did or have this emotional dysfunction that I had. I started sweating. I sat at the edge of my bed to catch my breath. I got up, and I went to the kitchen to get some water. I came back to my room, and I couldn't go to sleep, so I just sat up and started talking to God. I asked God, if he was to let me have this baby, for the baby to be ok and not have to live with this disorder. I began to have these thoughts of thinking the baby would come out with the same disorder, and I began to have doubts about having it. I didn't want the baby to go through what I went through and was going through. The bullying and ridicule that comes with this disorder, I didn't want them to face it. I prayed and talk to God until I fell back to sleep. I got up the next morning and called Rev. I needed to understand the dream I had the night before, and I needed to tell him the news. Remember, I mentioned earlier about the Prophet in our church that was praying and prophesying over the people. During my pursuit of knowing more about the encounters I was having, I gravitated to her. I wanted to learn and know more about the Holy Spirit and the prophetic. I was fascinated by her gift and the way she moved in the Holy Spirit. This particular Sunday they were having prayer. I was sitting the back of the church observing. As I

THE DARK SIDE THAT BIRTHED MY WORSHIP

was sitting in the back of the church, she calls for me to come to the front for prayer. I was shaking while walking to the front of the church. When I got to her, she began to pray in the spirit. I just stood there with my eyes closed. She whispered in my ear and began to tell me details of things I prayed and asked God about. I was in tears. She then said to me that my baby would not encounter it. I almost passed out. I couldn't believe what she was saying to me. She bent down and prayed over my ankles and then she came up my legs and stopped at my stomach. She prayed over the unborn child that was growing inside me. She came back up and laid her hands on me and said that just as I am unique, so shall this gift be unique but not as I think. Before I walked away, she whispered to me again and said, "She will not encounter it. My prayers and concerns were assured through the mouth of the prophet. Even though the enemy tried to convince me that my first born would have the same disorder, my God assured me through the mouth of the prophet that it is not so. This was a life-changing heartfelt assurance for something that had haunted me for weeks. I cried like a newborn baby. Nothing could have taken my joy in that moment. As I went to bed that night, I laid in the dark and began to replay what happened that morning in service in my head. And I just began to say, "Thank you, Jesus." It was like a river flowing. The next thing I remember, I woke up and the sun was shining. I had fallen asleep while praying in the Holy Spirit. After that night, I never wondered or worried about my baby and her future. I knew that she would not be born with this disease neither would her child. I believed from that day forth that the generational curse was broken. This disorder was broken off my children and their children. My senior year was going so fast. In spite of the shocking news of me being pregnant, I was still able to enjoy my last year of high school. While preparing myself to enter into adulthood, I was getting ready to have a little girl at the same time. I did everything I could to stay in school and graduate with honors. That day didn't come fast enough. I remember that day so vivid. It was at the Regal Theatre. I had to be at the school early, so I had to catch the bus. To give you a picture, I was eight months pregnant and I caught the bus to my graduation ceremony. Despite all I went through I wasn't going to let nothing stop me from getting there. Sitting there waiting for my name to be called. My emotions were all over the place. I didn't know if I was ashamed of walking across the stage while eight months pregnant, or if I was ashamed of the way my skin looked. As I was walking across the stage towards the principle

THE DARK SIDE THAT BIRTHED MY WORSHIP

all I could see was this big smile. I reach out my hand for the official handshake and I heard these words. Against it all you made it. I shook my head and said, "Yes I made it". Shortly after on July 13th, 1996. I gave birth to a healthy baby girl. In that moment I remember praying the entire time. My prayer was that she would love me beyond my imperfections, and that she sees me as God's see me. I became a mother at the age of eighteen. She made it all worth it. I was able to love someone that would love me back. I didn't have to wear this mask with her.

CHAPTER 13
JUST THE TWO OF US

My life started to seem normal. I was becoming a young adult. Closing that chapter of high school was a bittersweet. I had some fun times and met some amazing friends along the way, that ultimately outweighed the bad times. My pigment continued to fade away. By the time I graduated from High School, gave birth to my daughter, a large portion of the pigment in my face, arms and legs were gone. I was a mother now so I couldn't allow that dark side to overtake me any longer. I had to live for her. I had to be strong for her. I had to overcome the inner torment that consistently tried to overtake my mind. I had to live for her. That's what I did. I completely took the focus off of me and pour all my energy into her. I was in love with what God had given me. She was my world. There were a lot of people around me that helped me with her that I am grateful for. Even though I believe she was ok, I still would look into her eyes and wonder if she will have to face this monster that I had to live with. But this little voice in my mind would remind me otherwise. Sometimes at night, I would question if it was really Him speaking to me, but then something would happen that would tell me otherwise. I was still a member at our

THE DARK SIDE THAT BIRTHED MY WORSHIP

home church, by this time I was in the adult choir and very active in the youth ministry. I also was involved with the prophetic classes that the Prophet of the house was having. I wasn't like the others around the church, and I soon realized that early in my walk. I always tried to fit in but never seemed to. I began to dream again and more strongly, and they were getting to be so vivid. I began studying his word every night. Even though I was getting back to the place of seeking the things of God, there still was a part of me that wanted to fit in with what I thought was cool to be accepted by my friends. I was a young mother, and I did work and take care of my daughter, but I still wanted to be that girl that could still hang out and party. I was young, trying to find my way and figure out where I belong. Having this feeling and knowing deep down inside that I didn't belong, or there is something that is different about me besides my skin and the way I looked, ultimately still trying to fill a void. I knew I was searching for something but wasn't sure what it was. At one point, I thought I could do both. Another encounter with God was when the prophet called me up and I began to speak in this unknown language I thought to myself, "People are watching me and staring at my face." I thought about how all these eyes were looking at me. I drew back and closed my mouth. She hugged me and told me it was alright that in due time I would use this gift to change lives. I was so scared. I was shaking, and I began to cry. The prophet continued to say other things to me. One thing she said that sticks with me to this day. She told me that I would grow in the dark. "What does that mean?" I asked myself. "I will grow in the dark," were her words that kept ringing in my ears. I was so puzzled by that. As time went on and things began to happen with my daughter, I began to see what the prophetic word meant. This prophetic class was the cultivating moment that allowed my worship to grow and develop. It gave language to my worship which at that time I didn't know I had. I didn't know there was a language to worship. My daughter was growing, and things started to look so much better for us. Still living with my parents, it was me and her against the world. All my focus and energy were in protecting her from the ugliness of this world. Making sure she was ok. I endured a lot even after having my daughter living at home with my parents. My mother constantly reminding me of the mistake I made by having her as a teenager, but I kept enduring until I couldn't anymore. I started working for the city of Chicago. This was my first job after graduating from school. This job required me to travel to different city locations.

THE DARK SIDE THAT BIRTHED MY WORSHIP

Working at McDonalds downtown was one way I learned how to develop thick skin. I dealt with racism firsthand working downtown. The racism I encountered was not due to me being black but me being different. I thought I had dealt with the worst of people while working at McDonald's, but I hadn't. This was a different level of people I had to deal with working for the city. I was in what one would call the corporate world. I worked closely with executive and board members. Not only was I dealing with those that thought I was beneath them but to see me enter into an office and cause the entire meeting to stop and all eyes on me. The look of disgust was evil, to say the least. Because it was my job to communicate face to face with these people and pretend, they are not looking at me as if they saw a ghost was a horrible feeling, I had to do this every day. I found myself not having the confidence I thought I had when it came to speaking to them in these types of meetings. I remember praying so hard one night that God would allow people to see past my outer appearance and focus on the inner, focus on my intellect. This was my prayer. Although I thought I suppressed the little girl inside, I still dealt with her when she would try to come forth. I knew I was growing in God, that it was the enemy. It was my job to defeat this inner spirit by killing it with God's word and worship.

This darkness was the enemy that wanted me to ultimately die. I now was able to recognize that this dark place is where I would die if I continued to allow this little girl to overpower my mind. I also was at a place in my worship that I could speak the word of God and cause her to flee. I continued to pray this prayer that God will allow those that I come in contact with at work see the inner and not the outer appearance. A couple of weeks after, there was this big meeting and I had to present the portfolios to the clients in the meeting. I was going around the table to make sure everything was set up and one of the CEOs came into the room before it started. It was a woman and she spoke to me. I with my head down spoke back to her. I never looked up just continue to do what I was doing. She spoke again and asks me what my name was. I looked up but not in her face and told her my name. She walked over to me and said your Vitiligo is so unique. I stopped what I was doing and looked at her. She was a Caucasian lady with Vitiligo. I said to her how do you know what I have? She said, "because I have the same thing". I couldn't see it, so I ask her where? She came closer and held out her hands and arms. Then she turns her head to the side, and it was in her face on the right side. I was so amazed because I never saw anyone other than myself with my condition. Not only

THE DARK SIDE THAT BIRTHED MY WORSHIP

that, but for her to compliment me on my skin was very heartfelt. She began to share with me her story and I just sat there in Awe of all the things she was telling me. We had a lot in common because she shared many things that we both encountered. The meeting started and I had to leave, but before I left out of the room, she said these words "Walk with your head up with boldness and confidence because you are Beautiful". She said, "take it from me you can go all the way to the top". After that day I never saw that CEO again. That day another level of boldness and confidence was birthed inside of me.

CHAPTER 14
HOPE AGAIN
FINALLY LIBERATED

One day, I was walking down Madison in the downtown area of Chicago, going to one of the work sites, and there was this woman walking towards me. She was walking in my direction while looking right in my face. I remember looking down and looking back up, trying to figure out what she was looking at. I kept walking, and she was getting closer and closer. If anyone knows the traffic of the people in the downtown area, you have to keep a certain pace. You either walk fast or get run over by the traffic of the people. This lady was getting closer and staring right in my face. At this point I was getting irritated. By this time, I was in my early twenties. The pigment in my face was almost gone and my neck was fading. Both hands had completely lost pigment, and my elbows had turned as well. I would say 45 % of my body had lost its pigmentation. I still had not sought any further treatment or been to any doctor. As I said before I tried to suppress this part of my life so that I can live for my daughter. I wanted to give her a normal life and protect her from the ugliness of this world. In order for me to do that I couldn't focus on my skin and what it was doing. I tried to accept me for the

THE DARK SIDE THAT BIRTHED MY WORSHIP

uniqueness God made me as much as I could. I will never forget what the doctor told me and my parents. After all the test and consultations along with a million questions, he then said these words, "A cure has not been discovered". There has been extensive research done but no cure has been found. The actual cause has not been discovered either. This is something I never forgot. It was the one thing that stuck in my head since the age of twelve. This one statement shaped my thinking and my life. I will never go back to the original color of my skin. At this point, I stopped fighting to get my identity back. I stopped fighting to get my original look back. As I was walking down Madison Street, the lady still coming towards me, stops me right in my tracks and stood right in front of me. I did see her coming but when she got closer, I started to put my head down, didn't want her to notice that I knew she was looking at me. When I looked up at her, I noticed she had patches around her eyes. She reaches out to grab my hands, and I jump back, but then I notice around her nose and mouth she had small patches. She finally opened her mouth and spoke to me. She said, "You are so beautiful." I said "Thanks" and tried to go around her, but she continued to say, "I have never seen anyone of your culture with the same condition." She then went on to introduce herself and asked for my name. I told her my name and said it was nice to meet you still trying to walk away. The next thing she asks me was if I wouldn't mind sharing with her my story about my condition. I gave her the strangest look. In my mind, I'm thinking to myself, "Who are you"? "She must think I'm someone else." At this point, I didn't know if I should scream, run or snap off on this lady. I didn't know if I should punch her, cuss her out or just walk away. I was so stuck on the fact that she walked up to me and started touching me, asking me questions. I believe she sensed my vibe knowing I was in a rush she smiled and told me that she knew someone who specialized in Vitiligo. Now at this point, the enemy gets in my head, and anger began to rise. I said, "Lady, I don't know you, nor do I care to about a specialist." She looked at me and smiled again and then she chuckled. She apologized for being so forward. She proceeded to give me her doctor's information. She said this doctor worked at Northwestern Hospital, and she was a dermatologist that would be able to help me. I told her that I needed to get back to work. She gave me the dermatologist's card and said to call the office and make an appointment. She gave me her own card as well and told me to call her and let her know how it went. I was in such a hurry that it didn't really register right away what she said. After

THE DARK SIDE THAT BIRTHED MY WORSHIP

I got back to work at my desk, I pulled her card out and read it. My mind was racing with so many questions at this point. I replayed what she said to me about the doctor can help me with my Vitiligo. I kept asking myself what she meant by that. All I knew is that there wasn't a cure, so how could she help me. I was so puzzled. I didn't know how to process it. When I got home, I remember telling my mother about it. I told her I met a white lady that had the same skin disorder. I told her that she knew someone that could help me and make my skin turn back to the way it was. I told her the lady gave me her card, and she gave me the doctor's card. My mother kind of passively heard me. I believe she heard me, but it didn't register to her like it did to me. She really didn't hear my heart. My heart was saying that there is hope in curing me of this condition. This person was put in my path and gave me hope that I gave up on. My mother didn't turn me away, but she didn't seem enthused about it either. The feeling I had when I told her was like a kid who just got what they wanted for Christmas. The joy in my heart to know that I could be cured or a possibility that I could be healed and made normal again even at this age was indescribable. She didn't share that feeling with me. Maybe because she didn't understand, I don't know. Maybe because she had resolved that this was who I was and there was no hope. Remember, I never went back to the doctor, meaning my parents never took me to a doctor, specialist or anyone to help fight this disease. It could have been they didn't have the medical insurance to do so or they just didn't know what to do. I will never know. This moment for me gave me hope in my heart again. When I didn't get that response of hope from my mother, I decided to go for myself and not bother her about it anymore. At this point in my life, I was a young adult working with my own benefits, so it wasn't that I needed them to take me to the doctor, but it would have been nice to have her there for support. Whatever it was I was looking for from her, I never got in that moment. Next day, I went to work. I called and made an appointment with the dermatologist at Northwestern Hospital. I was so afraid, but I made the appointment anyway. I knew if I didn't make the appointment, I would always have the "What If" question playing in my mind. Every day after, on my work route, I would find myself looking for this lady. I called the number on her card, but she never picked up the call or returned my messages. This lady changed my life in a split second. I never saw her again. I had some many unanswered questions to ask her. She was the second Caucasian woman that had the same condition that cross my path.

THE DARK SIDE THAT BIRTHED MY WORSHIP

I never got the chance to ask the first lady any questions. As a matter of fact, I never met anyone other than them two with the same condition. I was not around others that had my condition at all. I was the only one in my school, neighborhood and family with Vitiligo. Being downtown, you get to see people from all walks of life, but I never saw one with Vitiligo. This lady and the other one had it, but the difference between me and her, skin complexion was white, so you could only see the patches if you were close to her. It's kind of looked like a birthmark. If she didn't point it out, I would not have noticed it. I mean I have seen those that were affected by Albinism, but no one with Vitiligo. So, this was such an experience for me because I met someone that looked like me to a certain extent. I had so many unanswered questions that I wanted to ask. I told my parents I made an appointment with the doctor. I ended up going to the appointment alone. I can recall the night before, I was in my room, and my mind was flooded with thoughts. The lady that saw me downtown seemed very convinced that this doctor had a cure for this disorder. I sat on my bed and wondered about all the what if's. What if my skin turns back to the way it was? What if I get sick? How would I feel? What would I say to my child when she gets old enough to learn the truth? What if there is no cure and they tell me what I was already told? How would I feel? So many thoughts came to my mind. I was getting so nervous and couldn't sleep. I finally fell asleep thinking about what all could happen the moment I go to see this doctor. I had a dream that night. It was a nightmare that caused me to wake up fighting. The dream seemed so real. In the dream, I was running down the street. It was dark and foggy. I came to some stairs while running I kept looking back. I started running down the stairs. I kept running and looking back as if someone was coming after me. I was running and all of a sudden, something grabbed me, and then I woke up fighting off what was grabbing me. It was like they were pulling me back into something, that I was fighting to get out. When I woke, it was pitch dark in my room. I was sweating and breathing so hard. It was like something was pulling me back trying to get me to go back into to something. This dream was so vivid. I couldn't shake the feeling. I was laying there trying to figure out what was going on. I closed my eyes and just meditated in song. I was telling myself God loves me. I got up to go to the doctor. On my way, I felt like I did when I went downtown as a little girl to try on the makeup that would cover up my skin. I had that same feeling all over again. I was nervous and scared at the same time. When I got to the hospital, I saw more people there waiting. There were people with other skin disorder and diseases there as well. I walked to the back to see the doctor. When I got to the back, I saw other Vitiligo patients that looked like I did. I was called into the room. The doctor began to examine me and looked at my skin. At first, she was looking at me as if she never seen someone with Vitiligo before. So, I was getting a little irritated because it seemed as if she didn't know what she was doing. Then she stated it always amaze her to see different patterns of Vitiligo on people in other cultures. She began to ask me all these questions. All related to the first time I went to the doctor in regard to my skin. After all that, she began to tell me of a treatment that can reverse the type of Vitiligo that I have. This treatment could cause my skin pigment to reverse and go back to its normal state. The doctor also told me that I could be one skin tone in time with this type of treatment. This treatment was a combination of an oral pill called psoralen in combination with UVB light therapy (photo chemotherapy). I would have to take the pill by mouth then I would undergo a UVB light. The doctor stated I would have to repeat this form of treatment up to three times a week for 8 to 12 months. In that moment, I literally felt a weight lift from the pit of my stomach. I felt as if all my nightmares were over. It was like my prayers were answered right in that moment. I was in such a place of shock that I was shaking. The treatment she was referring to would take longer to reverse the pigment because of the amount of pigment that had already been lost. She did go over other treatments, but she said this would be the best in my case. There was a part of me that was a little fearful. Once the doctor began to share the possible side effects the more I started to worry. She explained there would be a significant amount of UVB light radiation that I would have to have. To me it seemed extreme. Not only that but, there was a daily pill I would have had to take. This pill had its own set of side effects. The other thing was that the insurance I had did not cover the cost for the medication, because Vitiligo is considered to be a cosmetic condition. With the amount of lost pigment, I endured at the time, I would have had to take a minimum of 3 pills a day. One bottle of 30 pills was over a hundred dollars. Once the doctor went over everything; I sat there for a moment. I asked her one last question. I asked her, if I go through the treatment, would this completely reverse and cure this skin disorder, and would I be able to carry on with my life without any other treatment or long-term side effects? The last thing she said to me was that there is no guarantee that the Vitiligo would not come back, when she said that, it was like a bomb dropped and shattered my hopes and dreams. She saw the shift in my body language, and she said she would give me a moment to think about everything. She left the room, and I just sat there quietly. I could feel the tears flowing down my face. It was like that little girl that I thought I suppressed came and sat right on my lap. The room was getting so small, and I was there alone. Neither one of my parents were there to hold, hug me or wipe my tears. I sat there while this doctor tells me all over again that there was no cure. I would have to deal with this for the rest of my life. My heart was completely broken. Yes, there was a treatment but at what cost? The treatment included me taking radiation three times a week for months at a time. Not only that but, taking a pill at least three times a day. Not being able to be in the sun at all. Meaning I would have had to cover my entire body to protect my skin from getting skin cancer. Again, at what cost? Was it really worth it? I began to ask myself is it really worth it? In the beginning, I was ready to try it. I was ready to give it a go. Out of desperation, I was ready to try it. I was ready to go for it. Out of desperation it didn't matter the cost. The only thing that matter to me in that moment was for this curse to be reverse, but again at what Cost? The doctor came back in and asked me if I was okay. I told her I was. She then told me to go home and think it over. Maybe talk it over with my parents, then make another appointment when I was ready to come back to talk about a course of action. I walked out of that clinic with my heart in my hand. I went to the washroom and sat there in the stall. I could feel my emotions rising. I could feel the anger. I buried my face in my arms. I felt so ashamed and embarrassed. I didn't know who to be angry at, but I was. I was angry at the doctor, my parents, the lady that found me and most of all at myself. I was so angry at myself for allowing myself to believe. I had hope that the doctor was going to tell me something I needed to hear. I was mad at myself because I was in a good place mentally. I was working and building a life for myself and my daughter. I was getting to the place in God that allowed me to walk in the boldness and confidence from within. I was angry because I found my voice. I accepted the uniqueness of my skin. I was at the place where I wasn't afraid anymore. I wasn't ashamed. I didn't focus on the whispers and stares as much. I was in a good place. I learned how to worship my way through the emotional dysfunction. It seemed like when I walk out of her office; emotion and feeling that I thought I was free from came rushing back. As I was walking to the bus stop, it felt like I had bricks in my

THE DARK SIDE THAT BIRTHED MY WORSHIP

shoes. Suddenly, I felt like something pulled me back into this dark space that I was so far away from. Suddenly, insecurities and fear started to consume my mind. All this happened as soon as I left the hospital. The moment I walked out of that place; my mind was flooded with thoughts of never going to be healed. I was so angry. That lady came into my life and completely turned it upside down. She told me that this doctor could help me. She had me to believe there was hope. She told me these things, and I felt life inside of me because of what she said. "Why did she tell me that?" I kept asking myself. "Why did she come into my life at the time she did?" This was so puzzling to me because I was so confused. "Why did she stop me in the middle of downtown? Got my hopes up, for them to be crushed all over again by the mouth of the doctor?" I was so hurt I didn't know what to do. My self-esteem went so low. I got home and was greeted at the door by my daughter. I looked in the eyes of my little girl and just smiled. I held her so tight. I heard this voice tell me that she would never understand why her mother looked different from her. I knew right away that it wasn't God speaking to me. The devil knows how to attack you in your weakest moment. The spirit of discouragement tried to dwell within. I felt this power from within and I screamed so loud, "Nooo!!! Devil, you are a liar." I began to decree God's word

> *1 John 4:4 (NIV)*
> *You, dear children, are from God and have overcome them, because the one who is in you is greater than the one who is in the world.*

I declared His word, and what He promised

> *Deuteronomy 31:6 Be strong and courageous. Do not fear or be in dread of them, for it is the Lord your God who goes with you. He will not leave you or forsake you.*

I refused to let the enemy win. I was not allowing my mind to stay in that sinking place. I began to declare his word just as I learned to do. His word began to flow from my belly. It was so natural that I didn't hesitate, and I did not stop. I stood right in that hallway and began to worship my father. I was tired. I wanted peace. I needed the peace of God to overtake my mind in that moment. In that moment I felt the darkness was trying to overtake me and I had to shift. My eyes were closed and I was standing there holding my daughter worshipping God. My mother walked up and she saw me, I was in total worship. She stood there for a moment and then turned and went back to the kitchen. My mother never inquired about the doctor's visit and I never spoke about it nor did

THE DARK SIDE THAT BIRTHED MY WORSHIP

I ever go back to Northwestern Hospital. That was the end of me putting my hope in man. The way I felt when I left that office, I vowed to myself I will never feel that way again. I am the only one in my entire family that has this disorder. I was at the place where I was completely okay with that. I had my beautiful daughter to love, and she loved me back. I was at the place where I knew I had to live for her and nothing was going to take that away. I beat suicide and death. The enemy tried a few times to keep me in this place of bondage, but I refuse to allow him to occupy my mind and life any longer. The inner little girl that tried to convince me over and over again that I wasn't worth living, or that no one was going to love me for me, that little girl was buried forever. I was at the place where I loved myself past my pain. I was at the place in God where I knew how to pull from within to destroy the voice with God's word and with a melody of song that would bring me back from that dark side. Again, I was not going to take it anymore from the devil. In that moment, I was reminded of the day I received my first prophecy. She told me that God favored me and that He would make my name great. I began to say what David said in 2 Samuel 6:21 David retorted to Michal, "I was dancing before the LORD, who chose me above your father and all his family! He appointed me as the leader of Israel, the people of the LORD, so I celebrate before the LORD., "He chose me". These words were highlighted in mind. "God, you chose me." I began to declare it. "God, you chose me." That was my worship. I wasn't worried about anything in that moment. My mother from time to time would come from the back looking, but I didn't stop. I realize I was chosen to be the unique one in my entire family. He chose me to stand out everywhere I went. I realized in that moment of worship and prayer right in the hallway, I was chosen to be the example of who God is. I worshipped until my clothes came off in the spirit. My spiritual garments came off. The garments of torment, shame, hurt, rejection, pain, depression, and abandonment. Those garments I wore for years were holding me back, keeping me in fear. I worshipped God until they came off. That night, I never looked back. My worship became my testimony, the place where God let me know that I was chosen. My worship became my lifestyle. This was the place I stayed in. The dark side that once was the place where the little girl lived became an altar. I stood in that hallway for a long time holding my daughter and giving God my praise tears running down my face. I didn't know how long I was there and I didn't care. I finally got to a place where I went from the hallway to

THE DARK SIDE THAT BIRTHED MY WORSHIP

my room. I was never the same after that day. When I awoke the next morning to get my daughter ready for daycare and myself ready for work, it was like a birthing of something new had come over me. I didn't have the dreadful thoughts in the back of my mind. Those thoughts that I purposely tried to suppress daily were gone. It was like I was delivered right in that hallway. My mother didn't bother me or make me feel like what I was going was crazy. I never saw that lady that crossed my path. I never put my hope in doctors and man again. I accepted my uniqueness and never looked backed.

CHAPTER 15
MY LOVE STORY

A couple of years had passed since my experience with the dermatologist at Northwestern Hospital. I wasn't living in that reality anymore. It was resolved in my mind that I had a condition that was uncurable. The hope of me believing that one day it would change was gone from my heart. I took my focus completely off what I thought was my imperfections and put them on living. Not only for me but for my daughter. There were some nights I would find myself battling the torment of shame, doubt, and hurt of the reality, but I learned how to continue to suppress those emotions in God. With the help of those close to me, pushing me and protecting me when I was being attacked by the ignorance of the people, I was able to not stay in that broken place. God placed a couple of people in my life that were key to who I am today. There was a battle I was fighting, but it wasn't in my mind. This battle was the need to be treated like a daughter. The older I got the worse my relationship got with my mother. I continued to work and provide for my daughter, but it seemed like nothing was good enough for her love. By this time, I was working at the Chicago Police Department Headquarters. My route had changed, and I was

THE DARK SIDE THAT BIRTHED MY WORSHIP

no longer interacting with Executives. While working and taking care of my daughter, I was forced to leave my parents' home for some time. While doing so I was able to save enough money to get my own place. His hand was still upon me, and I never stopped going to my home church. I wanted to give my daughter the foundation I had. I made sure I took her to church. When I moved into my own place all I had was enough to move in. I was in a place where I couldn't allow myself nor my daughter to be hurt again. That night I was forced to leave my parents' home, I vowed to myself that I would never be put in this position again. I finally had my own. It was me and my daughter and a 13inch TV. That was all I had. It wasn't much but we had each other, and I could call it my own. The Vitiligo had continued to spread, and I was still encountering the stares and whispers of men. Nights were hard because it was just me and my daughter alone in an unknown neighborhood. I stayed faithful to God and my church. Every day on my route to work after taking my daughter to daycare, I would talk to this guy who worked at the train station. He was a very nice guy. He always asked about my daughter. He always offered to help if I ever needed anything. After some time went by, he asked me out on a date. I didn't take him seriously at first because we talked all the time. This time, he was serious. I decided to take him up on that date. We went out and had such an amazing time. We talked about a lot of things. He shared with me something I will never forget. One night he saw me standing by the train station alone late in the night with my daughter. I was standing there with tears flowing down my face. He asked me was I okay and I immediately told him I was fine. I walked off because I didn't want him to see me like that. He told me to hold up and ask me if he could walk with me. I told him it was okay. He insisted. That night he walked me to my god mother's house. This was the same night I was forced to leave my mother's home. He told me after that night he could not get me off his mind. He told me he prayed and ask God to allow him to love me beyond my hurt. He shared this with me on our first date and I never forgot it. This was the same night I prayed to God to send me a sign that I would make it through this pain. At first, I was worried he would be ashamed of me, but he wasn't. He made me feel really special. Something I had never felt with a man. Time went on and we talked and dated for a few months. One day he asked to come over to my place. I knew I didn't have anything in my place so I would make up some reason why he couldn't come over. Finally, one day I said yes and let him come over. I explained that I didn't have any furniture, he was ok with that. He came over, and we sat on the floor of my apartment and talked all night until it was time for him to go to work. The next time I saw him, he asked me to be his lady. This was a few months after just casually talking and dating. He never missed a beat with my daughter. He cared so much for her. He cared so much for me. He never treated me like I was a disease or a one-night stand. I endured a lot from a few men, so my focus was just my daughter and making a better life for her as a young mother. One day, I was home, he asked me if I mind him bringing a chair over to watch the game. I told him I didn't mind. The next morning, I left for work with my daughter and, when we got back home that evening, I opened my apartment door, and my place was fully furnished. I could not believe it. I called him to find out what happened. He told me that he could not let another day go by with my daughter sleeping on the floor. I didn't ask for it and I didn't do anything to deserve it. He was a genuine person that had a heart for me and my daughter. God knew what was needed at the time it was needed. As time went on our relationship grew and on December 16, 2000, he became my husband. He loved me beyond myself. It was not easy because I still from time to time dealt with the insecurities of true love. By the time I got married,

70% of my pigment was gone. I lost track of the progression of it. There were times we would be out and someone would walk up to me and ask me what happened, or if I was burned. It seemed like God would use him to say something to shift my emotion right in that moment. He would make me laugh and cry tears of joy to shake me out of that place of darkness that tried to creep in. People would even stare at us when we were out in public out of disbelief, he was with me. We shared a wonderful life together of 22 years and I am grateful every day because God put me in the place for him to find me. I was living for me and my daughter, but there was a void that I was still trying to fulfill. I still was looking for love in all the wrong places. I still had that need to be looked upon as a normal. Even though I was growing in my worship with God, I still was battling that inner torment that constantly tried to make me believe I would never live a full life free from the fear of rejection. God sent my husband Andre Wallace to fill that void I was searching for. He loved, encouraged, supported, protected, secured me and my daughter and he wiped every tear from my eye. When I had those moments of finding another patch or complain about my skin. He would hold me and tell me I love so you need to stop focusing on them and focus on me. He always told me I saved him,

THE DARK SIDE THAT BIRTHED MY WORSHIP

but he really saved me. Andre often told people he was my knight in shining armor and I would laugh and deny it. After looking back over the last 22 years of my life. He really was my Knight in Shining Armor. We raised three Beautiful children together and we never left each other side in doing so. He was our Superman. All though our Love Story didn't end as we planned. I will say this Fairytales do come true. My KING!!!

CHAPTER 16
NOW IT ALL MAKES SENSE

How did the dark side birth my worship? How can you become a worshipper in the dark? When you think about darkness it's not a place you would want to be. When you think of darkness, you think of blackness, dimness, shade, cloudiness, smokiness, gloom, shadows and obscurity. This is a place where little to no light exist. Well, how can one be in that place and God find them? How can life come from death? When you think of darkness, death generally comes to mind. If that is the case and if God is light, then how can one find light in darkness? According to

> **1 John 1:5 This is the message we heard from Jesus and now declare to you: God is light, and there is no darkness in him at all**

If God's word tells me here that in Him (God) there is no darkness at all, then how can He (God) who is light find a person in darkness? Psalms 23:4 declares it all. Even in your lowest and darkest time, God is with you. In my opinion, darkness does not always represent death or the place of no life. If you were to look deeper into what darkness can also represent, you would be completely enlightened. Darkness from a divine perspective can

THE DARK SIDE THAT BIRTHED MY WORSHIP

represent many things. From one perspective, it can represent the place of death, from another perspective it can represent a place of birth. When a mother is expecting a child, the fetus is being develop in the womb of the mother. If you look at it, this is the darkest place in the female. The womb represents life, where something is produced and formed. When you think of a fetus, the womb is where it grows, develops, and formed. The womb doesn't have light. You cannot see what's in the womb and all the parts that make it up with the naked eye. In order for you to fully understand how one can become a worshipper in the dark, I think it's important to look at this from a spiritual perspective.

> **Even in *Jeremiah 1:5 NLT Before I formed thee in the belly, I knew thee; and before thou camest forth out of the womb I sanctified thee, and I ordained thee a prophet unto the nations.***

The womb can symbolize a cave, dark and completely unseen. This womb is connected to the mother. While one is in the womb, they are receiving the vital things that are needed for you to grow and develop. In order for this the happen, you must stay connected to the source, which in this case is the mother. The fetus is not aware of this yet, it has to stay in the womb in order to live outside of the womb. Now we are not going to go into the full anatomy of the reproduction system when it comes to the birthing cycle of a baby, but I do want to point out a few key things. When you think about a womb and then think about the dark side of which I shared, this is where the birthing of my worship began. For many years, I looked at the dark side as the place where all the inner pain, hurt and anger of my heart were released and expressed. This was the place where the little girl would come forth and express herself. This little girl that I kept behind a wall would come forth. The dark side is the place where my spirit was at first being crushed. For a long time, I was slowly dying for who I was becoming on the dark side. Later as I began to have encounters with my Father in this same place, I was also being formed. My worship was being birthed in this same place of darkness. What do I mean by my worship was being birthed? What does it mean to be worshiper? The Bible says in

John 4:24 For God is Spirit, so those who worship him must worship in spirit and in truth.

In order to be a worshipper, one must worship him in spirit and in truth. In order for this to happen a dying and then a birthing must take place in order for the spirit man to be activated to become a worshiper. It becomes your lifestyle through his spirit. There is a lot

THE DARK SIDE THAT BIRTHED MY WORSHIP

of teaching on what it means to be a worshipper, but I can only share with you how I became one; a worshipper to the one and true living God. I was in a dark place and I had to come out of that place. The dark side was the womb that the worshiper was born out of. I was broken, torn, rejected, alone, scared, depressed, afraid and shameful of how I looked to the world. I didn't know how to express that in a way to be healed so I hid behind this wall. I developed this place of total darkness. I did not accept myself. All these emotions I kept hidden from the world was inwardly killing me. This little girl represented every emotion of a dark place you could think of, and she only made herself visible at night when no one was able to see, hear, or stop her. I want you to imagine a prison door before you, but it's so far away that you can't get to it. Imagine the moment you reached for the door, but it suddenly becomes so dim you can't see it anymore. Imagine this little girl in the dark, that is screaming to come out, but no one can hear her. She is calling out but no one comes. Once you have imagined this little girl, then I want you to call her by her name "LaToya". I was that little girl. That little girl lived in me. I would like to think she came along when the pigment disorder (Vitiligo) was discovered, but she was there all the time. We all have a dark side within us, we were all born with the nature of it. The key is how one comes from that dark side is what determines the path in life and ultimately your worship. It starts in the womb. How the dark side birthed my worship? It's really simple; I made a choice to surrender. God found me and pulled me out of the dark. I was so broken to the point of giving in. God purposed for me to live and pulled me from this place. Ultimately when I made the choice to surrender and give up the fight is when I was able to fully embrace me. I stopped fighting the little girl within. After the first encounter with God I was never the same. Before my first encounter and even more so after, I was fighting so hard that I was mentally exhausted. I was allowing myself to tune out everything and listen to that voice of darkness. Not knowing God was forming, shaping, and preparing me for the birthing. In my first suicide attempt, God showed me then He was with me, but I didn't see it. Even in the second attempt, He showed me He was there, but I didn't see it. I didn't hear His voice because I was on the dark side. The moment I surrendered and allowed my mind to not fight anymore, then is when I began to hear a different voice. That voice I began to hear over the other voices was God me pulling into the light. He was pointing me in the direction to where the light was so I could leave the dark side. God will send people in your life

THE DARK SIDE THAT BIRTHED MY WORSHIP

at the appointed time to speak to your inner man. After the first encounter, my inner spirit was awakened. I was able to hear with a different ear and didn't know. When I was giving in to the darkness, I was still able to hear. My outer ear wasn't hearing but the inner ear was. Eventually, I replaced my cry with prayer and song. I would replace my tears with smiles through worship. I would replace my language of rage and anger with divine tongues. The melody in my heart became my weapon. Early on, I didn't know how to fight. I wasn't taught the tools to fight. So, when this disorder began to show in my outer appearance, it was easy for the enemy to play with my mind. In the night before, I would lay there and I would allow the voices to consume my mind, but after the encounters and dreams, I learned a song, a melody that would bring me back and allow me to see the light. I knew as long as I stayed in that light, the little girl would be able to see the door and walk through it. Those melodies became a part of my heart and would arise to suppress the darkness. Those melodies became my prayers. When I received the evidence of the Holy Spirit by speaking in a divine language in the dark, I knew then that something was unique within me. I was communing with Him and not the voices in my mind. I began to sit with him and talk with him through prayer. Even when I found myself sinking, I would find my way back because the more I would sing and pray, the more I would come back from that place. Over time, God was molding me into a worshipper. This is what saved my life. This is how the worshipper was born. I simply chose to surrender, and I allowed my space to be filled with the love and light of God. Because I was in a space alone, I was able to learn how to tune out all the other voices and tune into His voice. This only happened the more I was alone with him. I got to a point where I wanted to just end my life and not have to deal with the reality that I was unique and that my skin was the evidence, but He didn't let that be. God wanted to show me how unique I was. He chose me. He literally pulled me out of the dark. When you meditate on something, it gets in your inner man, and it becomes a part of your identity. This is what my worship did for me. It became my identity. It caused me not to focus on the outside but the inside. Every night, I was in that place of darkness, But the more the little girl tried to overtake me with fear, shame, low self-esteem, silencing my voice, isolation, and loneliness, the more God revealed His self to me in unique ways. He saved me from myself. As I said before, some people look at the darkness as death, gloom, black, negative and just a place no one wants to be. Begin to look

THE DARK SIDE THAT BIRTHED MY WORSHIP

at your dark space from a different perspective. You will then see that it is a place where greatness can be birthed. A place where life begins and not end. A place where God shows you He is with you all along. A place where you surrender and give in and let go of the little girl or the little boy within you. I also know this to be true that the foundation of Church played a role in keeping me grounded in His word. The desire to know more of Him and to understand the things I was experiencing, was an open door for me to receive Him in my state of brokenness. Even though I had an amazing support system, through family, friends and love ones. I still had an inward battle I could only win with God. You often hear those who go into a dark place and never come out. They never come back from that place. You read and hear of people all the time in

Matt.4: 16 So, in the darkest place of my heart, a small flame was lit and got brighter and brighter.

Because of this light, I didn't end my life when I wanted to. Because of this light, I was able to come back from the dark place and live. I was able to find my voice and be the light in a dark place just as God tells us in His word. *(Matt. 5:16).* This was the time I got to know Him. The world is a cruel place and full of people who only see the outside beauty of a person. Beauty is a powerful component of one's identity. Only if people could see it from God's eye. If the inner beauty could overshadow the outer beauty, this world would be a better place. The mental and emotional stresses that many others endure because of it, would be better off. When low self-esteem is your dark place, find your inner beauty. When depression is your dark place, find the light that gives you joy (Nehemiah 8:10). When rejection is your dark place, find the light in God's love *(Proverbs 36:5-7)*. When abandonment is your dark place, find God's arms (Deut 3:18). This was the time my heart was humble and open. The Bible says *(scripture Psalms 51:17)*. My tears were my sacrifice. I was a little girl, broken and bruised and scared. My heart was scared because all I wanted was my life to be normal. God found favor in me. He spoke through the prophet and declared my future was secure. I will continue to pursue him. The life of a worshipper is a life devoted to Christ. The life of a worshipper is a life given to God. A life of a worshipper allows God to speak directly to you. I have encountered God in a miraculous way and because of it *The Darkside Birthed my Worship*. Because of it I am a conqueror. Because of it I am now able to take what I thought to be ugly and turn it into my beauty. I am Liberated. Now I can share my story, my journey and my victory

THE DARK SIDE THAT BIRTHED MY WORSHIP

of how a little girl who spent most of life living with a dark side overcame it. During that time, although my smile told those around me that I was fine and living with it. Now I can share how God patiently pulled me from it into His light. God did it and through my Faith in him, the love, care and support of my husband who pushed me to share my story and the cheerleading of my children I will no longer be silent. I am a Vitiligo Chic that has fully transformed. I am one of God's chosen vessels. If I could share my story to that one person that is facing their own form of darkness, I would tell them that God is light. I too was a victim to rejection, hurt, abuse, pain, low self-esteem, shame, depression, sickness, abandonment, feeling alone and unloved. Where suicide at one point, was my portion, but today I stand bold, beautiful and confident in who God has called me to be. Because he found me in my darkness, allow him to find you. As of today, 98% percent of my body has lost its pigment. Not only am I a worshipper, I also discovered my calling in the secret place of God as a prophet.

Sometimes we often reflect over the past years of our lives and wonder if we could change anything. One can sit for hours and pick apart the things they have faced and overcame in their past lives and play in the back of their minds what they would have done differently. I could remember the times I would sit and wonder how my life would be if I were a shade darker. Sometimes my mind would wonder if I had long hair and hazel eyes, maybe things would be different for me. If I were that girl, then my life would be easier. If I were that girl, then I would not have gone through all the pain I endured growing up. If I were that girl, maybe I would have had more opportunities available for me. Reflecting on if I was "THAT GIRL" I would have missed out on being God's chosen girl. My prayer is that through my testimony you will be set free from your dark side and begin to walk in the liberty of who God made you to be. God takes our "Beauty for Ashes".

www.ingramcontent.com/pod-product-compliance
Lightning Source LLC
Chambersburg PA
CBHW051401290426
44108CB00015B/2110